7
american popular piano
ETUDES

Compositions by
Christopher Norton

**Additional Compositions
and Arrangements**
Dr. Scott McBride Smith

T0078771

Editor
Dr. Scott McBride Smith

Associate Editor
Clarke MacIntosh

Book Design & Engraving
Andrew Jones

Cover Design
Wagner Design

A Note about this Book

Pop music styles can be grouped into three broad categories:

- **lyrical** — pieces with a beautiful singing quality and rich harmonies; usually played at a slow tempo;

- **rhythmic** — more up-tempo pieces, with energetic, catchy rhythms; these often have a driving left hand part;

- **ensemble** — works meant to be played with other musicians, or with backing tracks (or both!); this type of piece requires careful listening and shared energy.

American Popular Piano has been deliberately designed to develop skills in all three areas.

You can integrate the cool, motivating pieces in **American Popular Piano** into your piano studies in several ways.

- pick a piece you like and learn it; when you're done, pick another!

- choose a piece from each category to develop a complete range of skills in your playing;

- polish a particular favorite for your local festival or competition. Works from **American Popular Piano** are featured on the lists of required pieces for many festivals and competitions;

- use the pieces as optional contemporary selections in music examinations;

- Or...just have fun!

Going hand-in-hand with the repertoire in **American Popular Piano** are the innovative **Etudes Albums** and **Skills Books**, designed to enhance each student's musical experience by building technical and aural skills.

- **Technical Etudes** in both Classical and Pop Styles are based on musical ideas and technical challenges drawn from the repertoire. Practice these to improve your chops!

- **Improvisation Etudes** offer an exciting new approach to improvisation that guides students effortlessly into spontaneous creativity. Not only does the user-friendly module structure integrate smoothly into traditional lessons, it opens up a whole new understanding of the repertoire being studied.

- **Skills Books** help students develop key supporting skills in sight-reading, ear-training and technique; presented in complementary study modules that are both practical and effective.

Use all of the elements of **American Popular Piano** together to incorporate a comprehensive course of study into your everyday routine. The carefully thought-out pacing makes learning almost effortless. Making music and real progress has never been so much fun!

Library and Archives Canada Cataloguing in Publication

Norton, Christopher, 1953-

American popular piano [music] : etudes / compositions by Christopher Norton ;
additional compositions and arrangements, Scott McBride Smith ;
editor, Scott McBride Smith ; associate editor, Clarke MacIntosh.

To be complete in 11 volumes.
Publisher's nos.: APP E-00 (Level P); APP E-01 (Level 1); APP E-02 (Level 2); APP E-03 (Level 3); APP E-04 (Level 4); APP E-05 (Level 5).
Contents: Level P -- Level 1 -- Level 2 -- Level 3 -- Level 4 -- Level 5.
Miscellaneous information: The series is organized in 11 levels, from preparatory to level 10, each including a repertoire album, an etudes album, a skills book, a "technic" book, and an instrumental backings compact disc.

ISBN 1-897379-11-0 (level P).--ISBN 1-897379-12-9 (level 1).--ISBN 1-897379-13-7 (level 2).--ISBN 1-897379-14-5 (level 3).--
ISBN 1-897379-15-3 (level 4).--ISBN 1-897379-16-1 (level 5).--ISBN 978-1-897379-11-0 (level P).--ISBN 978-1-897379-12-7 (level 1).--
ISBN 978-1-897379-13-4 (level 2).--ISBN 978-1-897379-14-1 (level 3).--ISBN 978-1-897379-15-8 (level 4).--ISBN 978-1-897379-16-5 (level 5).--
ISBN 978-1-897379-17-2 (level 6).--ISBN 978-1-897379-18-9 (level 7).--ISBN 978-1-897379-19-6 (level 8)

1. Piano--Studies and exercises. I. Smith, Scott McBride II. MacIntosh, S. Clarke, 1959- III. Title. IV. Title: Études

MT222.N884 2006   786.2   C2006-906214-5

LEVEL 7 ETUDES

Table of Contents

Improv Etude - Bayou Tapestry

Module 1

Concept: 1st inversion & Dominant 7 chords

Triads may be written in **first inversion**. In a first inversion triad, the third of the chord is on the bottom. One way to change a root position triad to first inversion is to take the root off the bottom and put it on top.

A **Dominant 7 chord** (also known as a 7 chord) combines a major triad (e.g., D-F♯-A) with a minor 7th above the root (e.g., C♮). Sometimes this is done using all four notes (e.g., D-F♯-A-C♮), but often it is done with only three notes to achieve the same sound.

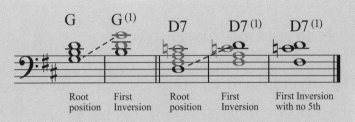

7 chords may also be written in **first inversion**. In a first inversion 7 chord, the third of the chord is on the bottom. One way to change a root position 7 chord to first inversion is to take the root off the bottom and put it on top.

A Label the first inversion triads and 7 chords with their lettername (e.g., G, D, or D7) and a bracketed 1 for "first inversion". Practice the left hand first *without*, then *with* the backing track.

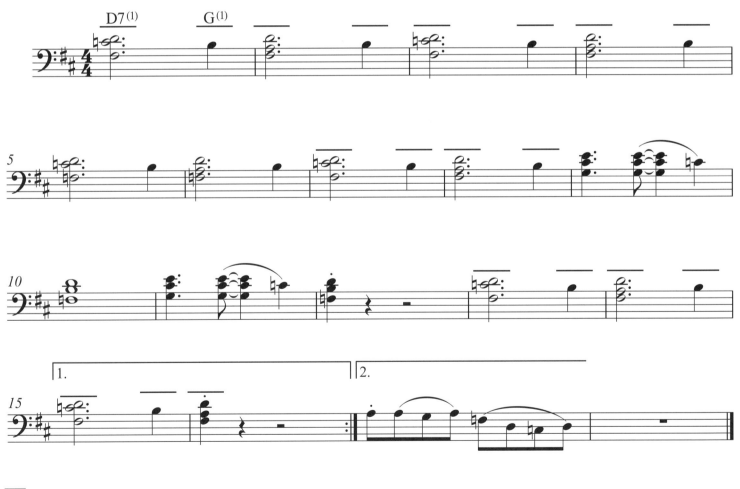

B Tap this rhythm while counting out loud; repeat until memorized. Then tap the rhythm with your right hand while playing the chord progression with your left. Finally, make up your own rhythms to go with the left hand chord progression.

© Novus Via Music Group Inc. 2009. All rights reserved.

Improv Tools

To improvise on *Bayou Tapestry*, you will use the **D Blues scale**.

One way to describe the **Blues scale** is as a **minor pentatonic** with an added lowered 5th scale degree. In this way, the **D Blues scale** would be described as a D **minor pentatonic** (D, F♮, G, A, C♮) with an added lowered 5th scale degree (A♭).

D Blues scale

There are specific Improv Tools you can use to make your scale-based improvisation interesting and musical.

Call & Response: play an idea, then "answer" it with a contrasting idea:

Grace Notes: liven up your improvisation with grace notes:

C Using the Improv Notes Set as indicated in the score, play various right hand improvisations. Use the Improv Tools, above, to get started. Practice *with* the backing track.

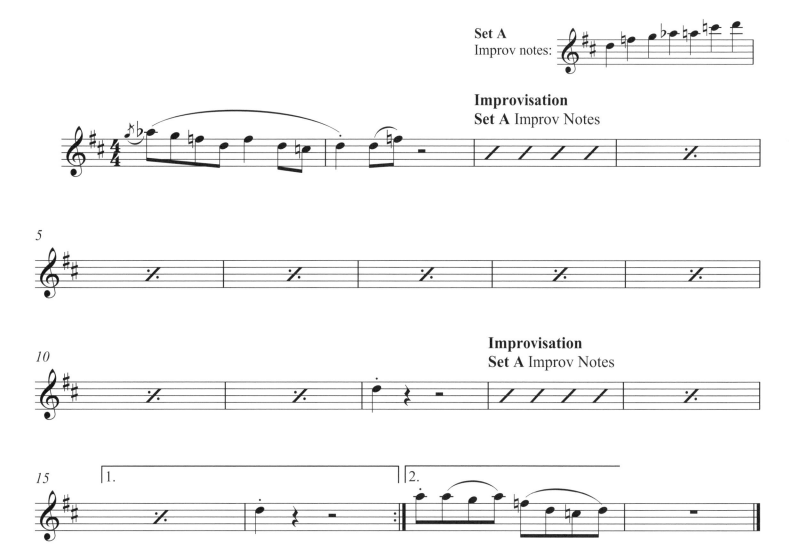

© Novus Via Music Group Inc. 2009. All rights reserved.

4

D Now improvise hands together. Practice first *without*, then *with* the backing track.

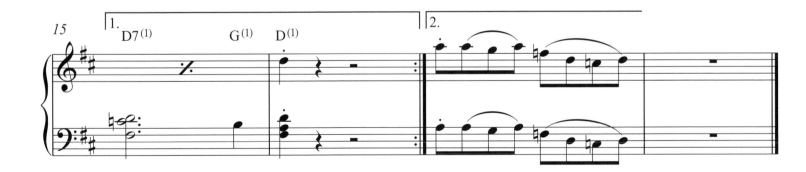

✔ **Improv Tip:** *Short phrases, with rests between them, can be very effective in "blues" solos.*

© Novus Via Music Group Inc. 2009. All rights reserved.

Vamping Tools

Vamping is an improvised accompaniment style. It often features repeated patterns based on blocked chords or broken chords in the right hand against single notes in the left hand.

You can vary right hand blocked chords in several ways:
Vamp Idea 1 – a long chord followed by a rhythm:

Idea 2 – a rhythm with the bass, then syncopated to it:

Idea 3 – the reverse order of the rhythms from Idea 2:

E Vamp various right hand accompaniments using the chords [in brackets] indicated below. Use the Vamping Tools, above, to get started. Practice first *without*, then *with* the backing track.

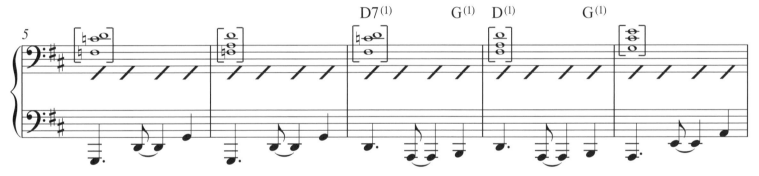

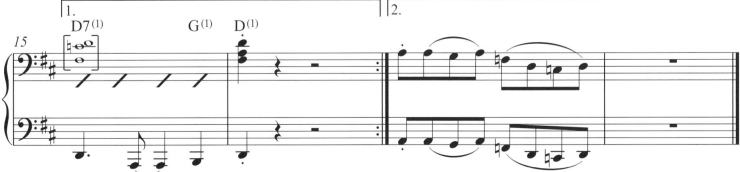

© Novus Via Music Group Inc. 2009. All rights reserved.

Improv Etude - Bayou Tapestry

Module 2

Concept: Dominant 7 chords

A **Dominant 7 chord** (also known as a 7 chord) combines a major triad (e.g., A-C♯-E) with a minor 7th above the root (e.g., G). Sometimes this is done using all four notes (e.g., A-C♯-E-G), but often it is done with only three notes to achieve the same sound.

7 chords may be written in **third inversion**. In a third inversion 7 chord, the minor seventh of the chord is on the bottom. One way to change a root position 7 chord

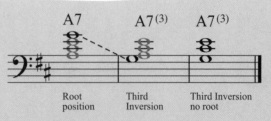

to third inversion is to take the 7th off the top and put it on the bottom. When only three notes are used to play a third inversion 7 chord, it is usual to omit the root.

A Label the third inversion 7 chords with their lettername (e.g., A7 or G7) and a bracketed 3 for "third inversion". Practice the left hand first *without*, then *with* the backing track.

B Tap this rhythm while counting out loud; repeat until memorized. Then tap the rhythm with your right hand while playing the chord progression with your left. Finally, make up your own rhythms to go with the left hand chord progression.

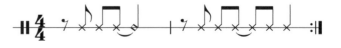

© Novus Via Music Group Inc. 2009. All rights reserved.

Improv Tools

Idea & Variation is another Improv Tool you can use, as well as **Call & Response** and **Grace Notes**.

Improvisations can also use arpeggio-based ideas.

Call & Response: play an arpeggio-based idea, then "answer" it with a contrasting idea:

Grace Notes: can be particularly effective for the style of a "blues" piece:

Idea & Variation: play an idea and then repeat it with a slight variation (even by only one note!):

C Using the Improv Notes Set as indicated in the score, play various right hand improvisations. Use the Improv Tools, above and in the previous Module, to get started. Practice *with* the backing track.

© Novus Via Music Group Inc. 2009. All rights reserved.

8

D Now improvise hands together. Practice first *without*, then *with* the backing track.

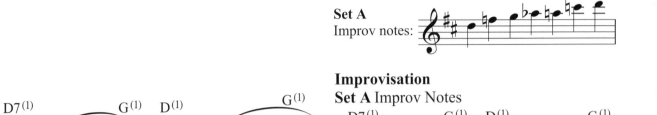

Improvisation
Set A Improv Notes

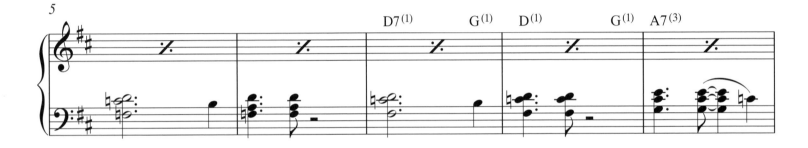

Improvisation
Set A Improv Notes

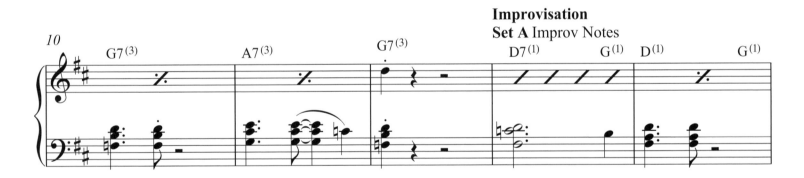

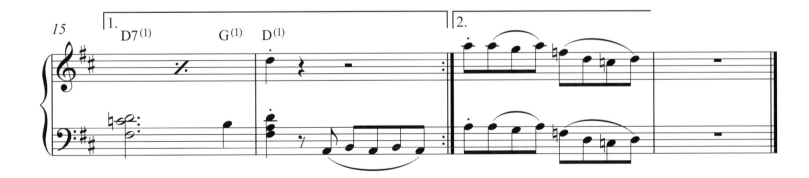

✔ **Improv Tip:** *Improvised melodies need a definite shape. Some sections should have a feeling of greater movement, others less.*

© Novus Via Music Group Inc. 2009. All rights reserved.

Vamping Tools

Vamps can also use broken chords in the right hand. You can create interest by varying the starting note of the arpeggio.

Vamp Idea 1 – start from the bottom note of the chord:

Idea 2 – start from the top note of the chord:

Idea 3 – start from the middle note of the chord:

E Vamp various right hand accompaniments using the chords [in brackets] indicated below. Use the Vamping Tools, above and in the previous Module, to get started. Practice first *without*, then *with* the backing track.

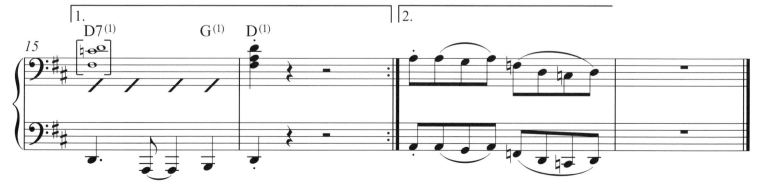

© Novus Via Music Group Inc. 2009. All rights reserved.

Improv Etude - Bayou Tapestry

Module 3

Concept: major 6 split chords

A **major 6 chord** (also known as a 6 chord) combines a major triad (e.g., F-A-C) with a major 6th above the root (e.g., D). Sometimes this is done using all four notes (e.g., F-A-C-D) or sometimes it is done using only three notes to achieve the same sound.

Split chords can occur when playing chords with both hands. A split chord has a Bass note in the left hand that is not the root of the chord – sometimes it is not a note from the chord at all. The top chord of a split chord may be a 6 chord.

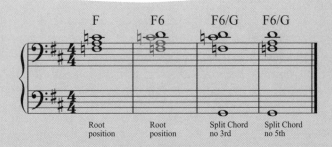

In the *Bayou Tapestry* improvisation, the "G" bass note is played in the backing track, creating a split chord sound in relation to the left hand chord.

A   Label the 6 split chords with their lettername (e.g. F6/G).
Practice the left hand first *without*, then *with* the backing track.

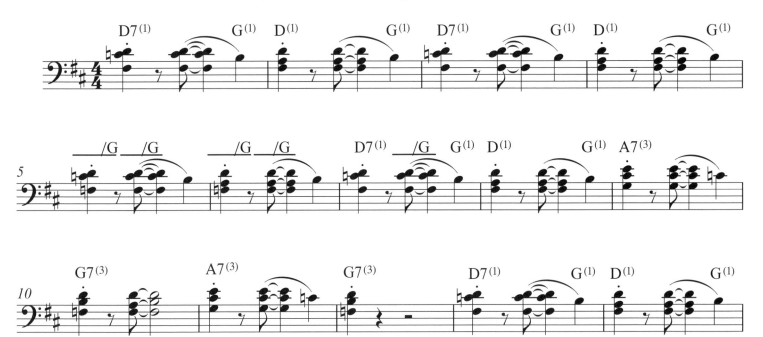

B   Tap this rhythm while counting out loud; repeat until memorized. Then tap the rhythm with your right hand while playing the chord progression with your left. Finally, make up your own rhythms to go with the left hand chord progression.

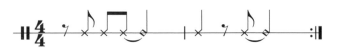

© Novus Via Music Group Inc. 2009. All rights reserved.

Improv Tools

There are other Improv Tools you can use to add color and interest to your improvisation. These Tools can be used with either scale-based or arpeggio-based ideas.

Pedal Notes: a pedal note is a repeated note that doesn't change when the melody moves. Here, the D's are pedal notes "above" the melody:

Tremolo: often used by blues players. Experiment with playing them fast or slow to see which works for you:

Continuous run: play a running stream of continuous eighth notes:

C Using the Improv Notes Set as indicated in the score, play various right hand improvisations. Use the Improv Tools, above and in the previous Modules, to get started. Practice *with* the backing track.

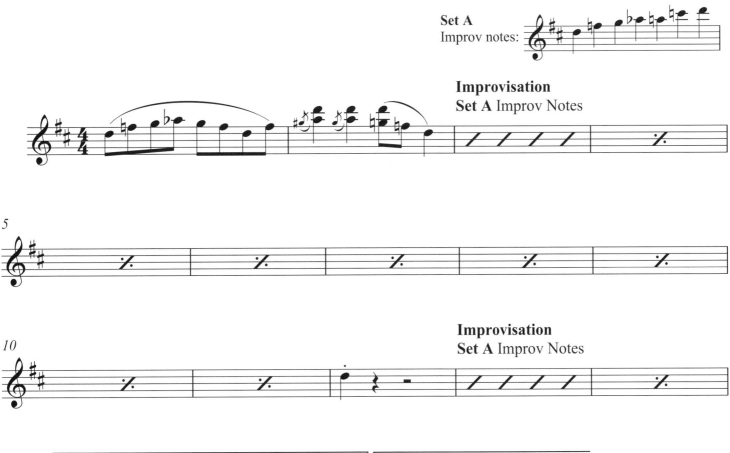

© Novus Via Music Group Inc. 2009. All rights reserved.

12

D Now improvise hands together. Practice first *without*, then *with* the backing track.

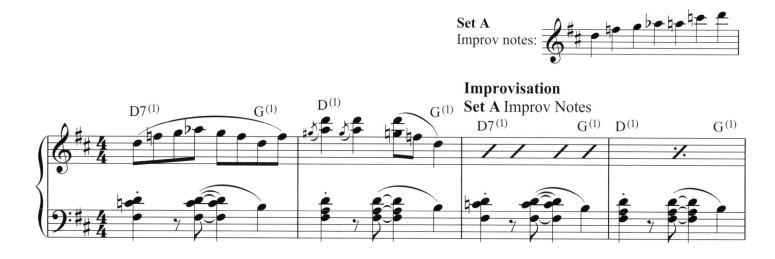

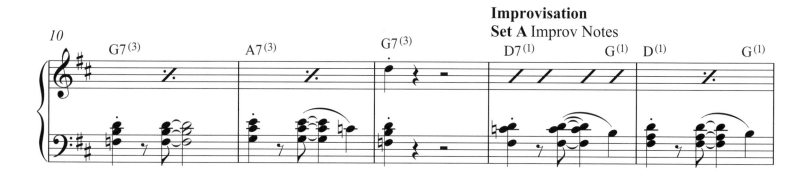

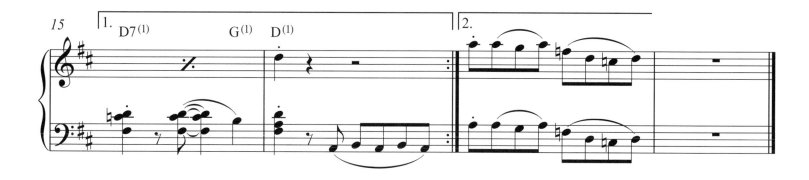

✔ **Improv Tip:** *Play a short phrase several times. Each time add one or two more notes.*

© Novus Via Music Group Inc. 2009. All rights reserved.

Vamping Tools

You can use a mix of blocked and broken chords in your vamp.

Vamp Idea 1 – an arpeggio followed by blocked chords:

Idea 2 – a long blocked chord followed by an arpeggio:

Idea 3 – syncopated blocked chords followed by an arpeggio:

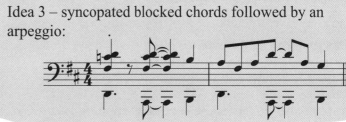

E Vamp various right hand accompaniments using the chords [in brackets] indicated below. Use the Vamping Tools, above and in the previous Modules, to get started. Practice first *without*, then *with* the backing track.

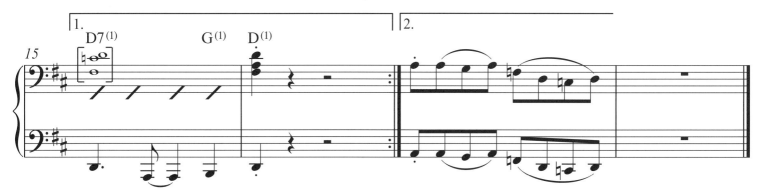

© Novus Via Music Group Inc. 2009. All rights reserved.

Improv Etude - Cruising Along

Module 1

Concept: second inversion

A triad is a three note chord. A **root position triad** in **close position** is written line-line-line or space-space-space. A chord takes its name from the bottom note of the chord in root position, called the **root**.

Triads may also be written in **second inversion**. In a second inversion triad, the fifth of the chord is on the

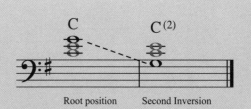

bottom. One way to change a root position triad to second inversion is to take the top note and move it to the bottom.

A Label the root position and second inversion triads with their lettername and a bracketed 2 to indicate "second inversion", where appropriate. Practice the left hand first *without*, then *with* the backing track.

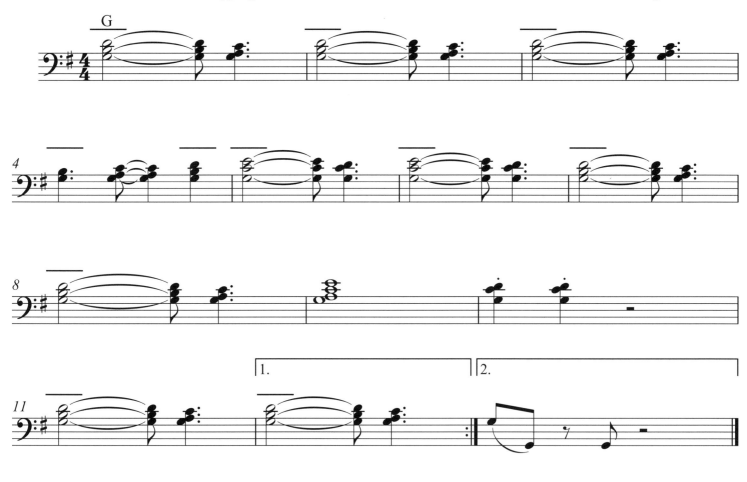

B Tap this rhythm while counting out loud; repeat until memorized. Then tap the rhythm with your right hand while playing the chord progression with your left. Finally, make up your own rhythms to go with the left hand chord progression.

© Novus Via Music Group Inc. 2009. All rights reserved.

Improv Tools

Improvisations often use scale-based ideas. To improvise on *Sparkling*, you will use an Improv Notes Set based on the **G major pentatonic scale**.

One way to describe the **major pentatonic** is as a major scale without the 4th or 7th notes. So, the **G major pentatonic** would be: G, A, B, D, E, G, leaving out the C and the F♯.

G major pentatonic

There are Improv Tools you can use to make your improvisation interesting and musical.

Idea & Variation: play an idea and then repeat it with a slight variation:

Pedal Notes: a pedal note is a repeated note that doesn't change when the melody moves. Here the D's are pedal notes "above":

C Using the Improv Notes Set as indicated in the score, play various right hand improvisations. Use the Improv Tools, above, to get started. Practice *with* the backing track.

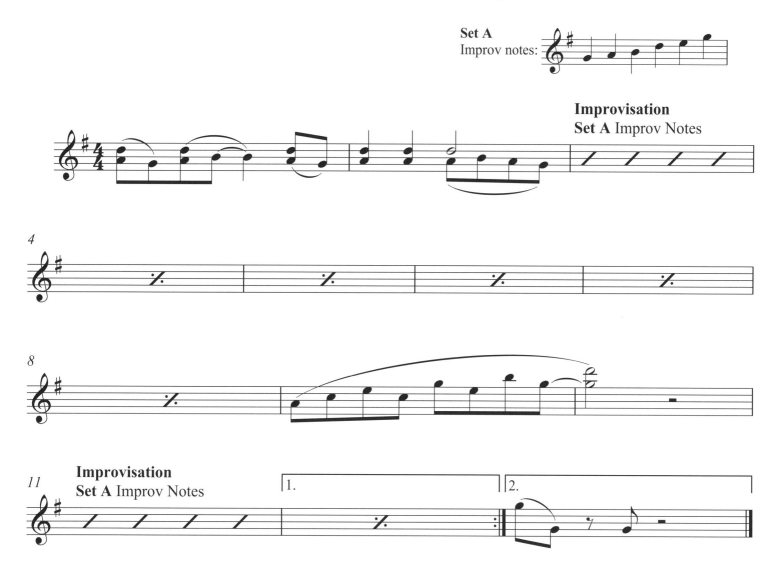

© Novus Via Music Group Inc. 2009. All rights reserved.

D Now improvise hands together. Practice first *without*, then *with* the backing track.

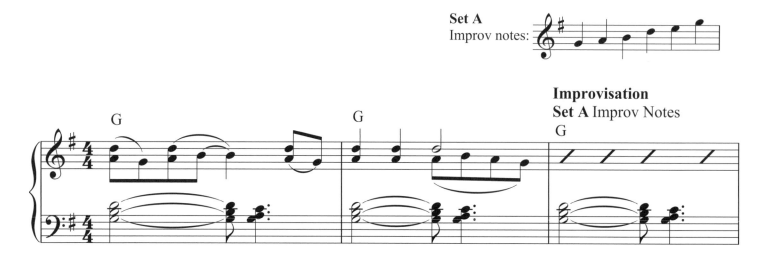

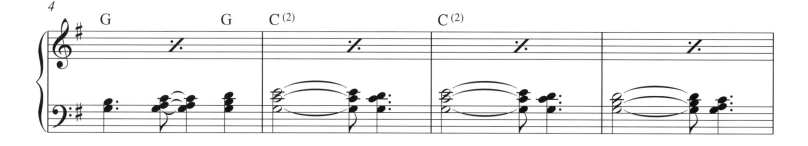

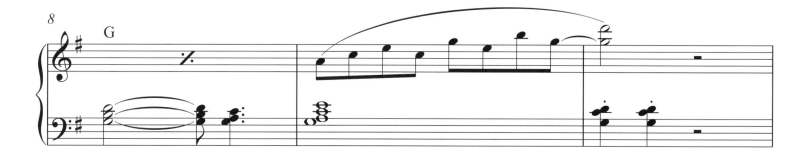

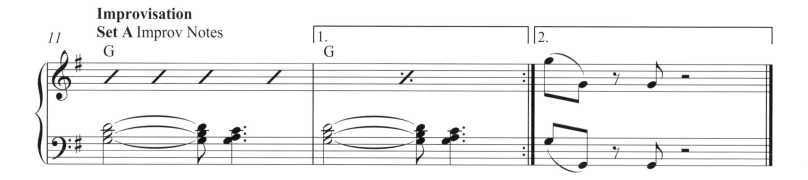

✔ **Improv Tip:** *Don't be afraid to play the same one or two notes over and over – the effect as the chords change underneath can be very good!*

© Novus Via Music Group Inc. 2009. All rights reserved.

Vamping Tools

Vamping is an improvised accompaniment style featuring repeated chord patterns in the right hand against single notes in the left hand. You can vary blocked right hand chords by changing the rhythms.

Vamp Idea 1 – match the rhythm guitar in the backing track, then play a longer chord in the next measure:

Idea 2 – reverse mm. 1 & 2 from the first pattern:

Idea 3 – play along with the rhythm guitar throughout:

E Vamp various right hand accompaniments using the chords [in brackets] indicated below. Use the Vamping Tools, above, to get started. Practice first *without*, then *with* the backing track.

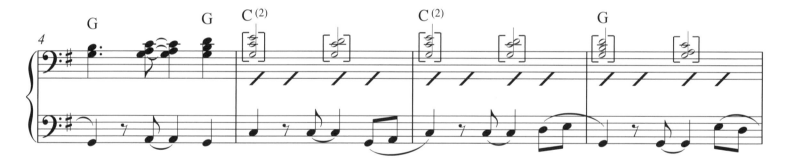

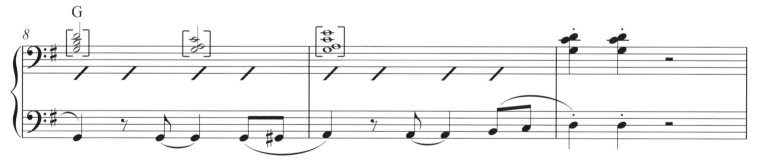

© Novus Via Music Group Inc. 2009. All rights reserved.

Improv Etude - Cruising Along

Module 2

Concept: minor 7 chords

A **minor 7 chord (m7)** combines a minor triad
(e.g., A-C-E) with a minor 7th above the root (e.g., G).
This is the same construction as the 7 chord, only based
on a minor triad.

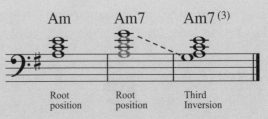

Minor 7 chords may be written in **third inversion**. In a
third inversion m7 chord, the minor 7th of the chord is
on the bottom.

One way to change a root position m7 chord to third
inversion is to take the 7th off the top and put it on
the bottom.

For improvising on *Cruising Along*, the 5th of the
Am7 chord may be omitted.

A Label the m7 chords with their lettername (e.g., Am7) and a bracketed 3 for "third inversion".
Practice the left hand first *without*, then *with* the backing track.

B Tap this rhythm while counting out loud; repeat
until memorized. Then tap the rhythm with your
right hand while playing the chord progression
with your left. Finally, make up your own rhythms
to go with the left hand chord progression.

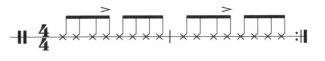

© Novus Via Music Group Inc. 2009. All rights reserved.

Improv Tools

Grace Notes is another Improv Tool you can use, in addition to the **Idea & Variation** and **Pedal Notes**.

Pedal Notes: a pedal note is a repeated note that doesn't change when the melody moves. Here both the G's and D's are used as pedal notes "above":

Idea & Variation: play an idea and then play a variation of the idea:

Grace Notes: embellish your improvisations with grace notes:

C Using the Improv Notes Set as indicated in the score, play various right hand improvisations. Use the Improv Tools, above and in the previous Module, to get started. Practice *with* the backing track.

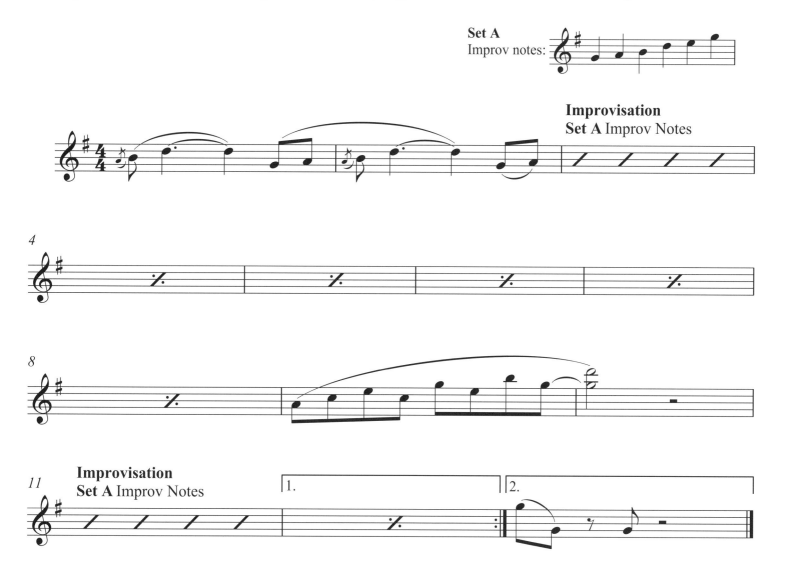

© Novus Via Music Group Inc. 2009. All rights reserved.

D Now improvise hands together. Practice first *without*, then *with* the backing track.

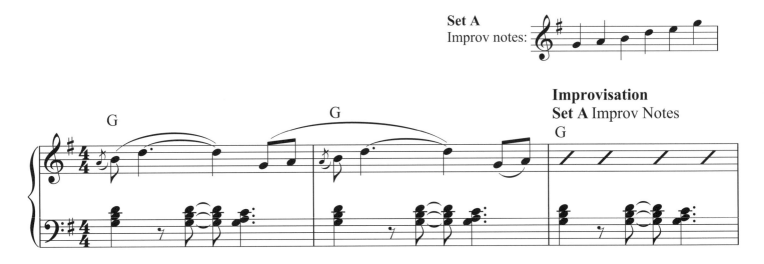

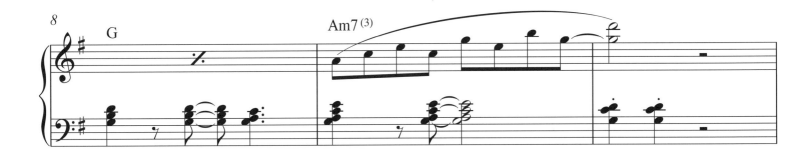

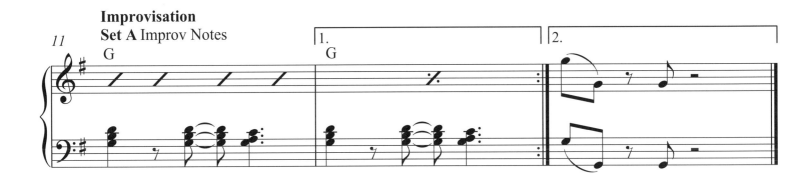

✔ **Improv Tip:** *Listen closely to the left hand chords – you can play more notes in the right hand when the left hand is resting or playing long notes.*

© Novus Via Music Group Inc. 2009. All rights reserved.

Vamping Tools

Your vamp can also use broken chords in the right hand.

Vamp Idea 1: an arpeggio figure starting on the bottom note:

Idea 2: an arpeggio figure that starts at the top:

Idea 3: an arpeggio figure starting in the middle:

E Vamp various right hand accompaniments using the chords [in brackets] indicated below. Use the Vamping Tools, above and in the previous Module, to get started. Practice first *without*, then *with* the backing track.

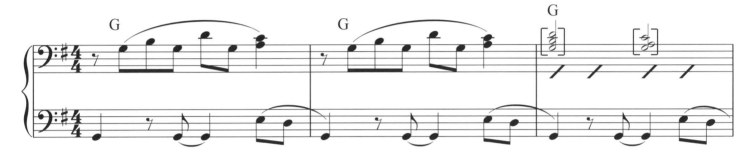

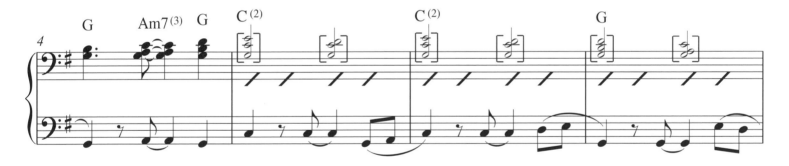

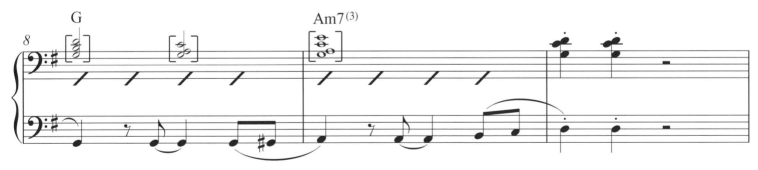

© Novus Via Music Group Inc. 2009. All rights reserved.

Improv Etude - Cruising Along

Module 3

Concept: sus4 chords

A suspension **sus4 chord** (also known as a **sus chord**), is created when the fourth degree of a scale is used in a chord instead of the third degree, "suspending" the resolution we expect to hear.

A suspension can be applied to any chord. To change a root position **7 chord** to a **7sus chord**, take the third degree of the scale and move it up to the fourth degree. Just like 7 chords, 7sus chords may be written in **first inversion**. One way to change a root position

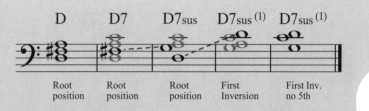

7sus chord to first inversion is take the root off the bottom and move it to the top.

For improvising on *Cruising Along*, the root of the 7sus chords will be left out, using only three notes to achieve the same sound.

A Label the first inversion 7sus chords with their lettername (e.g., D7sus) and a bracketed 1 for "first inversion". Practice the left hand first *without*, then *with* the backing track.

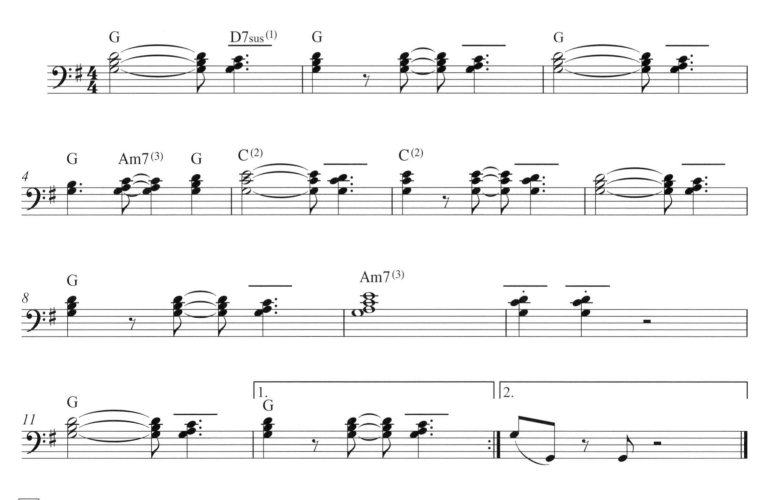

B Tap this rhythm while counting out loud; repeat until memorized. Then tap the rhythm with your right hand while playing the chord progression with your left. Finally, make up your own rhythms to go with the left hand chord progression.

© Novus Via Music Group Inc. 2009. All rights reserved.

Improv Tools

There are other Improv Tools you can use to "spice up" your improvisation.

Direction Change: play an idea and then send it back the other way:

Call & Response: "answer" an idea with a contrasting idea:

Rhythmic Shift: play an idea and then re-state it starting on a different beat:

C Using the Improv Notes Set as indicated in the score, play various right hand improvisations. Use the Improv Tools, above and in the previous Modules, to get started. Practice *with* the backing track.

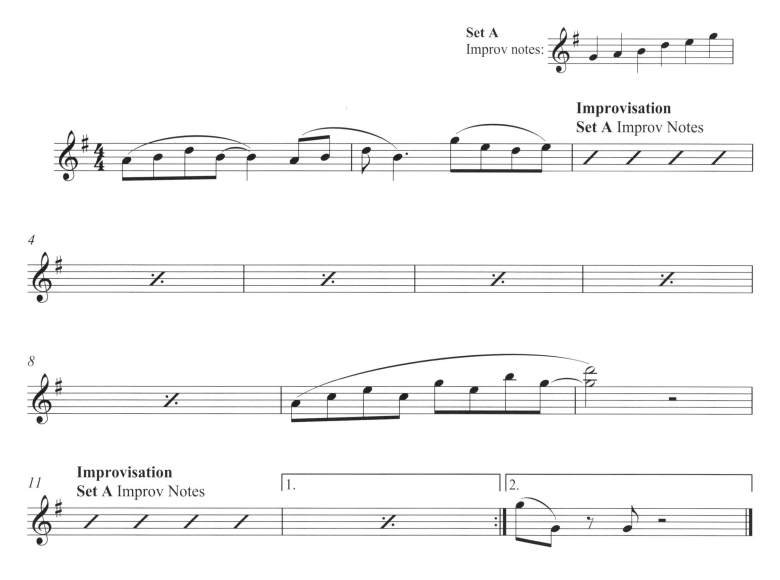

© Novus Via Music Group Inc. 2009. All rights reserved.

D Now improvise hands together. Practice first *without*, then *with* the backing track.

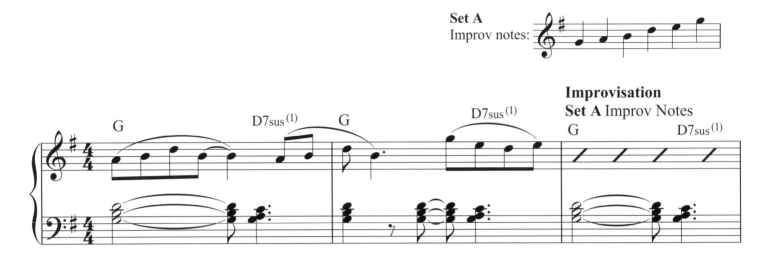

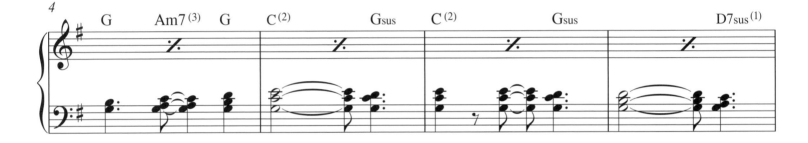

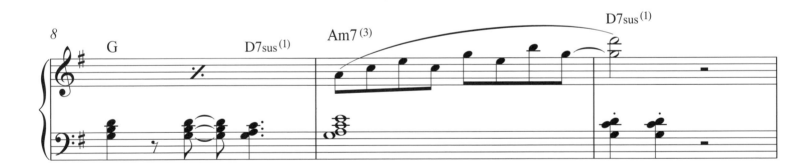

✔ **Improv Tip:** *In a song with very little harmonic tension, try using Rhythmic Shift to create interest in your improvisation.*

© Novus Via Music Group Inc. 2009. All rights reserved.

Vamping Tools

Your vamp can use a combination of blocked and broken chords in the right hand. Here are three stimulating options.

Vamp Idea 1:

Idea 2:

Idea 3:

E Vamp various right hand accompaniments using the chords [in brackets] indicated below. Use the Vamping Tools, above and in the previous Modules, to get started. Practice first *without*, then *with* the backing track.

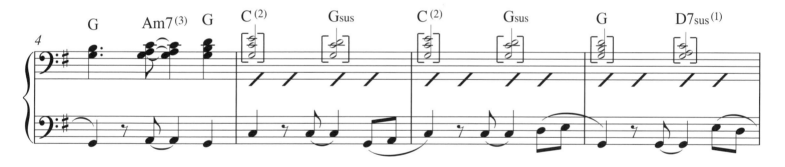

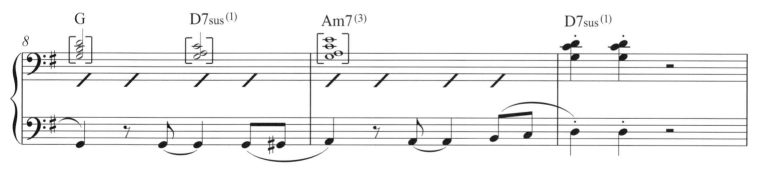

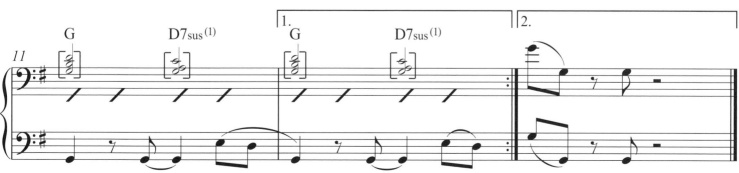

© Novus Via Music Group Inc. 2009. All rights reserved.

Improv Etude - Lonely Waltz

Module 1

Concept: 7, major 7 & minor 7 chords

A **dominant 7 chord** (also known as a 7 chord) combines a major triad (e.g., A-C♯-E) with a minor 7th above the root (e.g., G).

A major 7 chord (**maj7**) is also based on a major triad (e.g., G-B-D), but adds a major 7th above the root to the chord (e.g., G-B-D-F♯).

And a **minor 7 chord (m7)** combines a minor triad (e.g., A-C-E) with a minor 7th above the root (e.g., G).

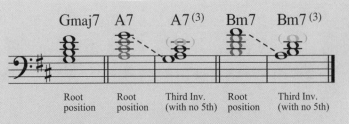

All 7 chords may be written in **third inversion**. In third inversion 7 and m7 chords, the 7th (i.e., the minor 7th above the root) is on the bottom.

For improvising and vamping on *Lonely Waltz*, the 5th of the 7, maj7, and m7 chords will be left out.

A Label the 7, maj7, and m7 chords with their lettername (e.g., A7, Gmaj7, or Bm7) and a bracketed 3 for "third inversion" where appropriate. Practice the left hand first *without*, then *with* the backing track.

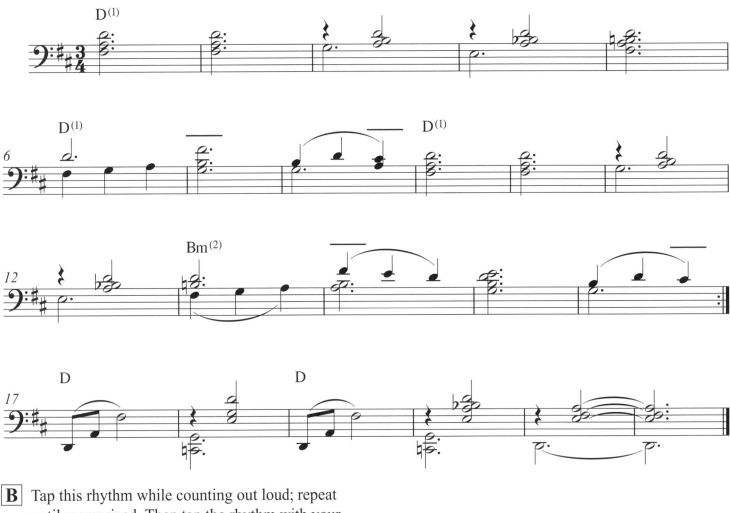

B Tap this rhythm while counting out loud; repeat until memorized. Then tap the rhythm with your right hand while playing the chord progression with your left. Finally, make up your own rhythms to go with the left hand chord progression.

© Novus Via Music Group Inc. 2009. All rights reserved.

Improv Tools

To improvise on *A Lonely Waltz*, you will use two different sets of Improv Notes: one based on the **A Mixolydian mode**, the other based on the **G melodic minor scale** (ascending).

One way to describe A Mixolydian is as an A Major scale with a G♮ instead of a G♯. Lowering the 7th degree of any major scale by a half step changes it into a Mixolydian mode.

Here are two Improv Tools you can use to make your improvisation more interesting and musical.

Call & Response: play a scale-based idea and then "answer" it with another:

Direction Change: create a scale-based idea that goes up, then down – or down, then up:

A Mixolydian mode

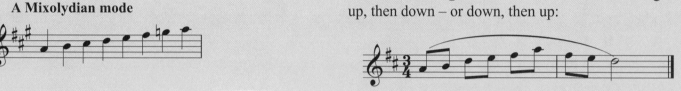

C Using the Improv Notes Set A or B as indicated in the score, play various right hand improvisations. Use the Improv Tools, above, to get started. Practice *with* the backing track.

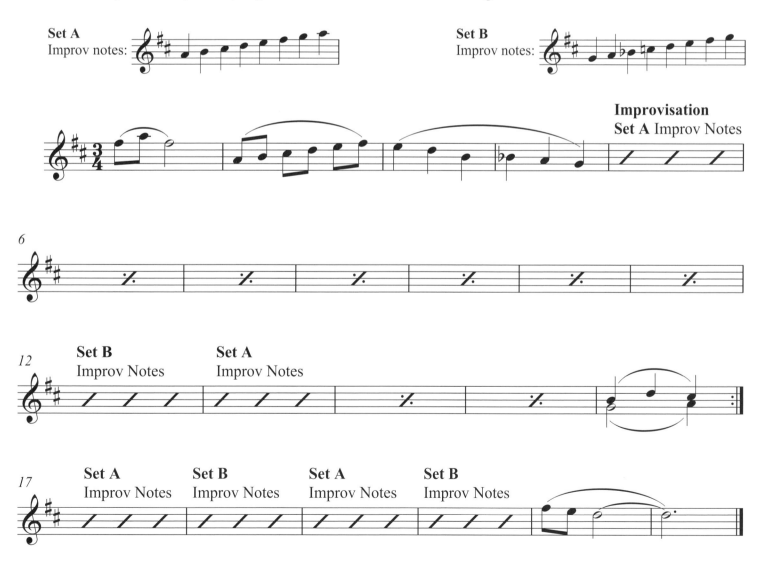

© Novus Via Music Group Inc. 2009. All rights reserved.

D Now improvise hands together. Practice first *without*, then *with* the backing track.

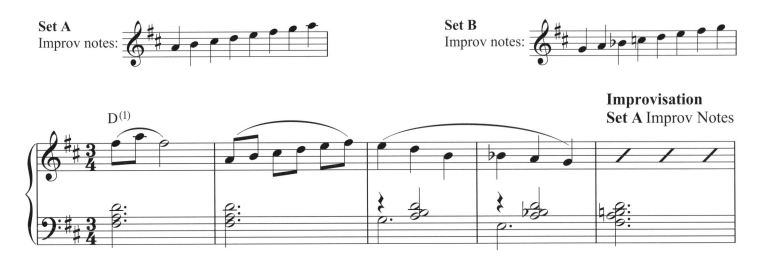

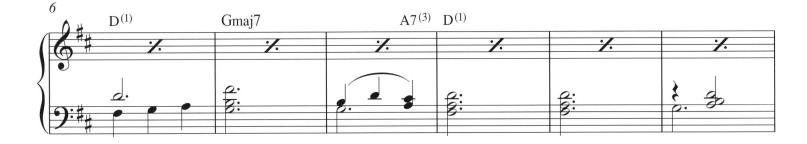

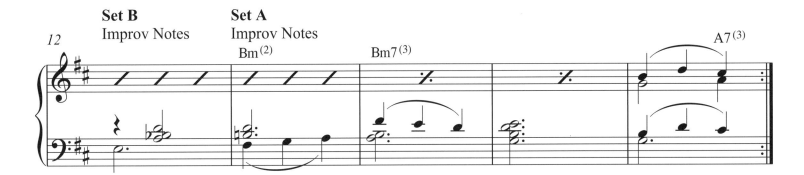

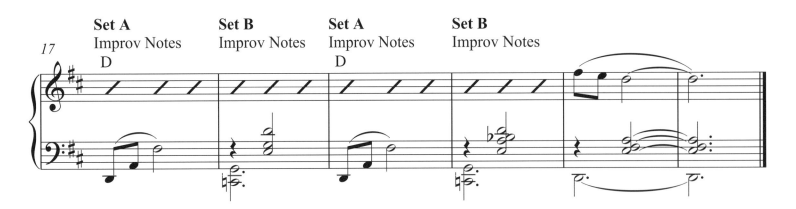

✔ **Improv Tip:** *Include motifs from the written-out melody in your improvisation. This will give your performance a feeling of unity.*

© Novus Via Music Group Inc. 2009. All rights reserved.

Vamping Tools

Vamping is an improvised accompaniment style often featuring chords in the right hand against single notes in the left hand. When vamping with blocked chords in the right hand, you can use various rhythmic patterns and syncopations to create interest.

Vamp Idea 1 – quarter note right hand chords:

Idea 2 – partially broken and blocked chords:

Idea 3 – use sustained chords when the bass line moves:

E Vamp various right hand accompaniments using the chords [in brackets] indicated below. Use the Vamping Tools, above, to get started. Practice first *without*, then *with* the backing track.

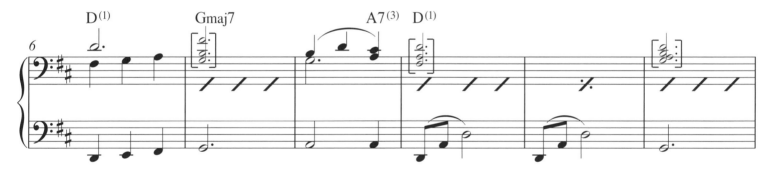

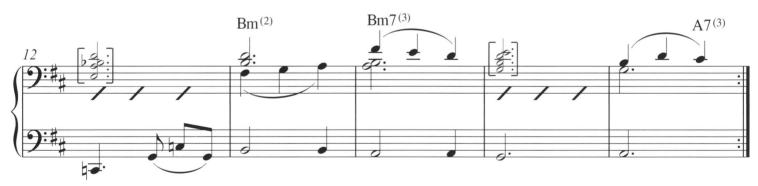

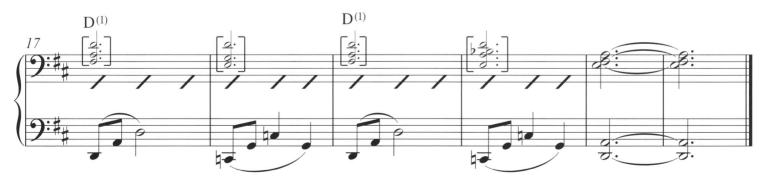

© Novus Via Music Group Inc. 2009. All rights reserved.

Improv Etude - Lonely Waltz

Module 2

Concept: major 6 & split chords

A **major 6 chord** (also known as a 6 chord) combines a major triad (e.g., D-F♯-A) with a major 6th above the root (e.g., B). Sometimes this is done using all four notes (e.g., D-F♯-A-B) or sometimes it is done using only three notes to achieve the same sound. In **first inversion** 6 chords, the third is on the bottom.

Split chords can occur when playing chords with both hands. A split chord has a bass note in the left hand that is not the root of the chord – sometimes it is not a note from the chord at all.

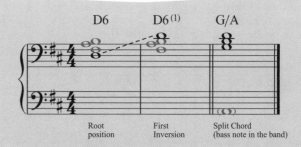

In the *Lonely Waltz* improvisation, the "A" bass note of the split chords is played in the backing track, creating a split chord sound in relation to the left hand chord.

A Label the 6 and split chords with their lettername (e.g., D6, G6, or G/A) and a bracketed 1 for "first inversion" where appropriate. Practice the left hand first *without*, then *with* the backing track.

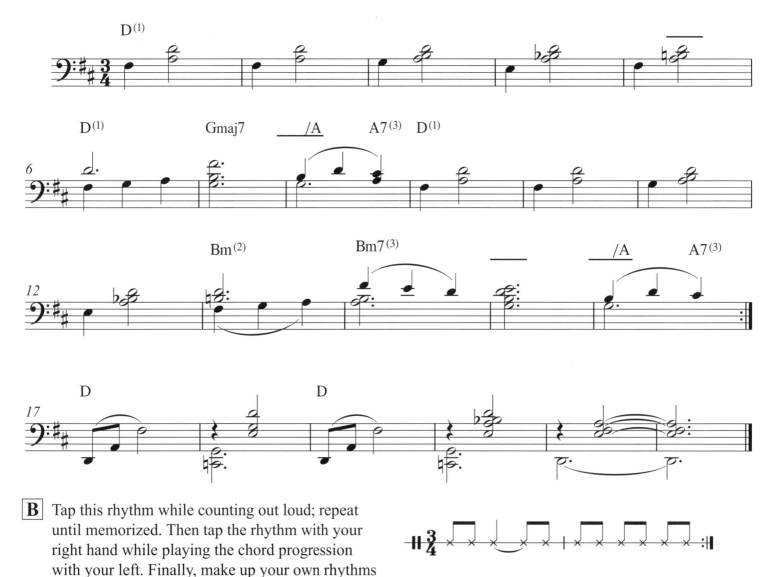

B Tap this rhythm while counting out loud; repeat until memorized. Then tap the rhythm with your right hand while playing the chord progression with your left. Finally, make up your own rhythms to go with the left hand chord progression.

© Novus Via Music Group Inc. 2009. All rights reserved.

Improv Tools

Idea & Variation is another Improv Tool you can use, in addition to Call & Response and Direction Change. Your improvisation can also use arpeggio-based ideas.

Call & Response: play an arpeggio-based idea and then "answer" it with a contrasting idea:

Direction Change: play an arpeggio-based idea, then turn it back the other way:

Idea & Variation: play an arpeggio-based idea and then repeat it with a slight variation:

C Using the Improv Notes Set A or B as indicated in the score, play various right hand improvisations. Use the Improv Tools, above and in the previous Module, to get started. Practice *with* the backing track.

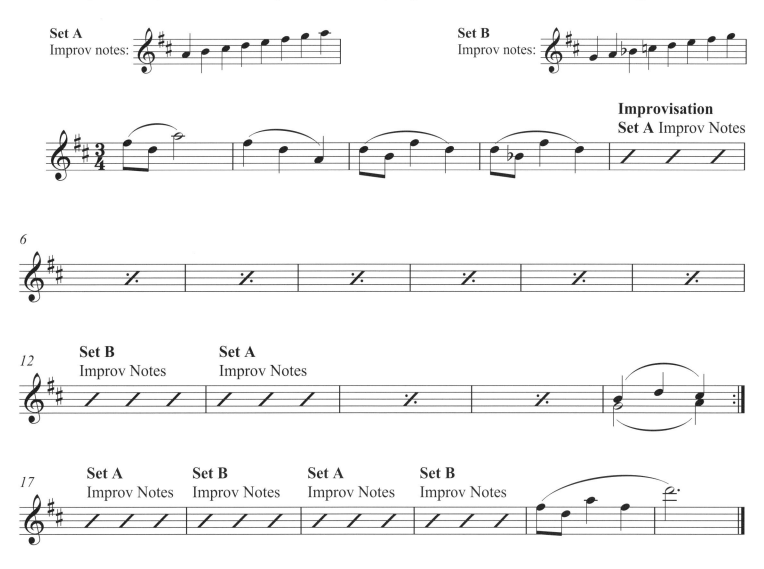

© Novus Via Music Group Inc. 2009. All rights reserved.

D Now improvise hands together. Practice first *without*, then *with* the backing track.

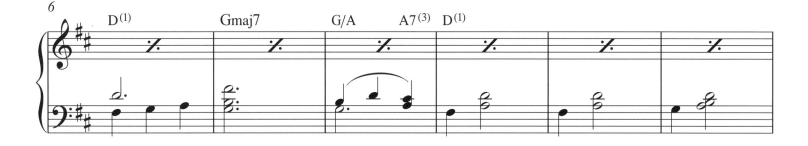

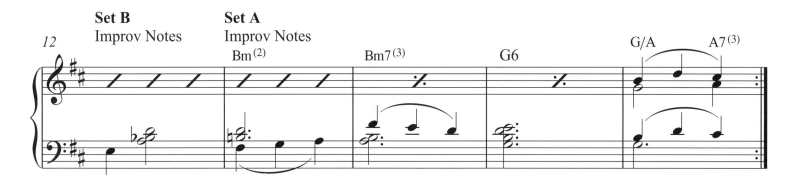

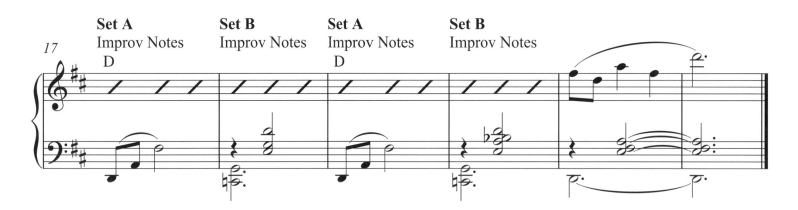

✔ **Improv Tip:** *In the sections where you use Improv Notes Set B, try to feature the notes that are different from Set A.*

© Novus Via Music Group Inc. 2009. All rights reserved.

Vamping Tools

Vamps can also use broken chords in the right hand. You can create interest by varying the starting note of the arpeggio.

Vamp Idea 1 – start from the bottom note of the chord:

Idea 2 – start from the top note of the chord:

Idea 3 – start from the middle note of the chord:

E Vamp various right hand accompaniments using the chords [in brackets] indicated below. Use the Vamping Tools, above and in the previous Module, to get started. Practice first *without*, then *with* the backing track.

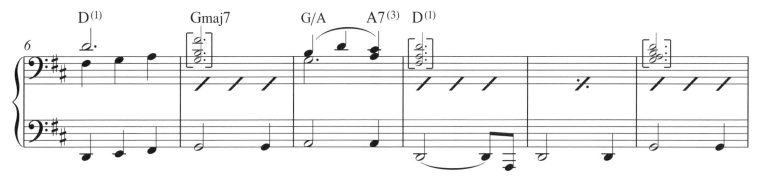

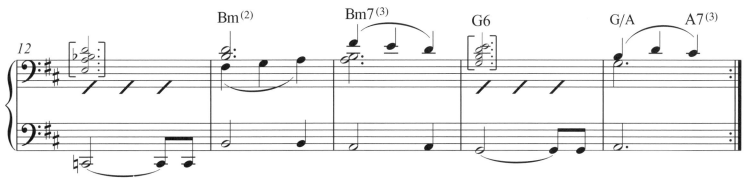

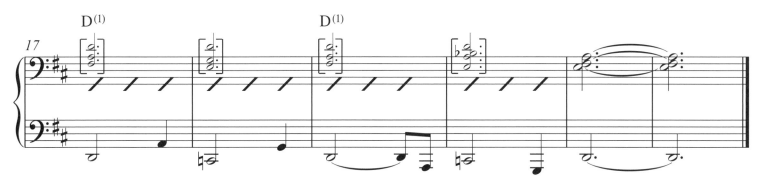

© Novus Via Music Group Inc. 2009. All rights reserved.

Improv Etude - Lonely Waltz

Module 3

Concept: 13 & add9 chords

A **13 chord** extends a dominant 7 chord by adding a 9th, 11th, and 13th to the chord (e.g., C-E-G-B♭-D-F-A). Often this is done using fewer notes to achieve the same sound, usually omitting the 11th and sometimes the 5th.

Similarly, a 9 chord adds a 9th above the root to a 7 chord. When the 7th is to be left out, this is indicated by saying the 9th is "added". So, a **Dadd9** chord adds a 9th, without the 7th, to a G major triad (D-F♯-A-E).

13 and add9 chords may be written in **first inversion**. In a first inversion chord, the third of the chord is on the

bottom. Add9 chords may also be written in **fourth inversion**. In fourth inversion, the ninth of the chord is on the bottom. One way to change a root position add9 chord to fourth inversion is to take the 9th off the top and put it on the bottom; you'll also lose the root or move it up an octave.

A Label the 13 and add9 chords with their lettername (e.g., C13, Cadd9, Gadd9, or Dadd9) and a bracketed "1" or "4" for the inversion, as appropriate. Practice the left hand first *without*, then *with* the backing track.

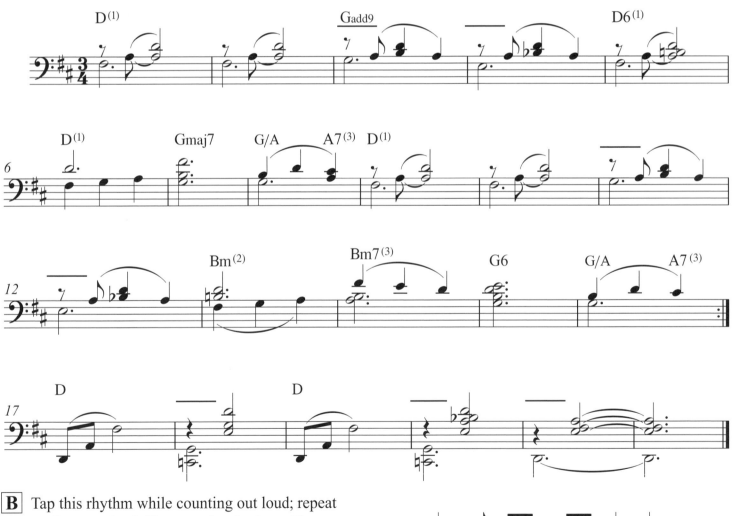

B Tap this rhythm while counting out loud; repeat until memorized. Then tap the rhythm with your right hand while playing the chord progression with your left. Finally, make up your own rhythms to go with the left hand chord progression.

© Novus Via Music Group Inc. 2009. All rights reserved.

Improv Tools

There are other Improv Tools you can use to add color and interest to your improvisation. These Tools can be used with either scale-based or arpeggio-based ideas.

Pedal Notes: a pedal note is a repeated note that doesn't change when the melody moves. Here the A's are used as pedal notes "above":

Chording: play chords in both hands as a great way to create rich effects in an improvisation:

Thirds & Sixths: harmonize your melodies with a mixture of thirds and sixths:

C Using the Improv Notes Set A or B as indicated in the score, play various right hand improvisations. Use the Improv Tools, above and in the previous Modules, to get started. Practice *with* the backing track.

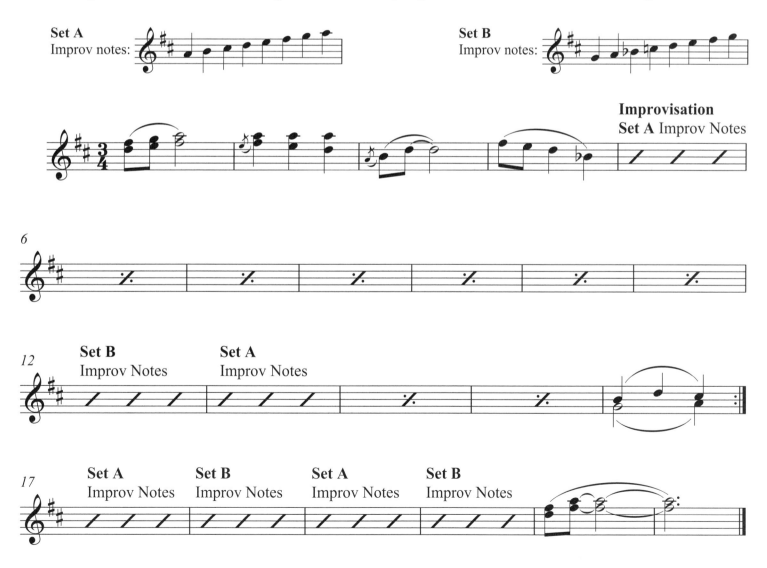

© Novus Via Music Group Inc. 2009. All rights reserved.

D Now improvise hands together. Practice first *without*, then *with* the backing track.

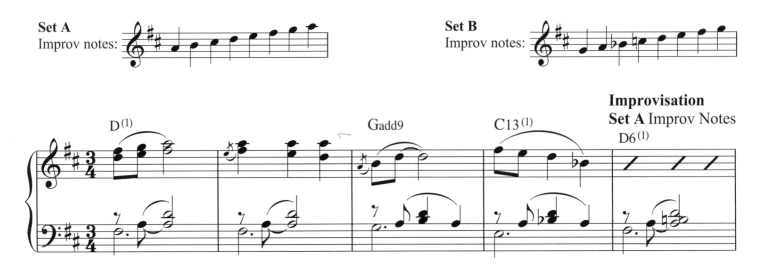

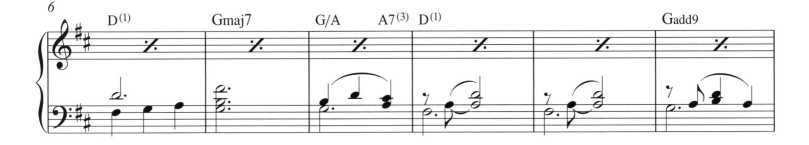

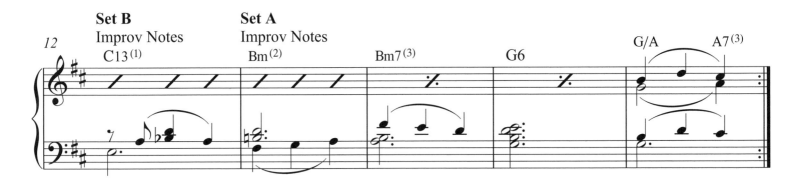

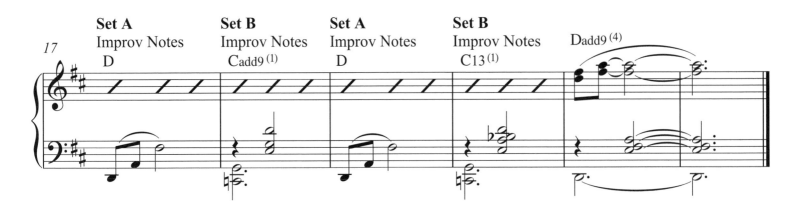

✔ **Improv Tip:** *Try Chording, playing chords in both hands, throughout your improvisation.*

© Novus Via Music Group Inc. 2009. All rights reserved.

Vamping Tools

Here are three more vamping ideas for *Lonely Waltz* which combine blocked and broken chords. You can adjust your right hand pattern to complement changes in the left hand bass line.

Idea 2:

Vamp Idea 1:

Idea 3:

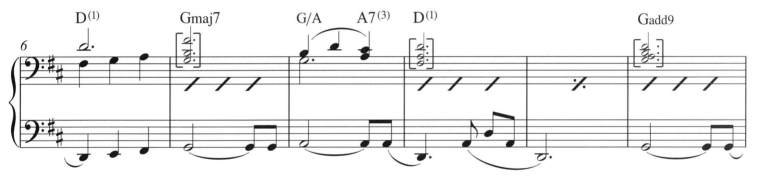

E Vamp various right hand accompaniments using the chords [in brackets] indicated below. Use the Vamping Tools, above and in the previous Modules, to get started. Practice first *without*, then *with* the backing track.

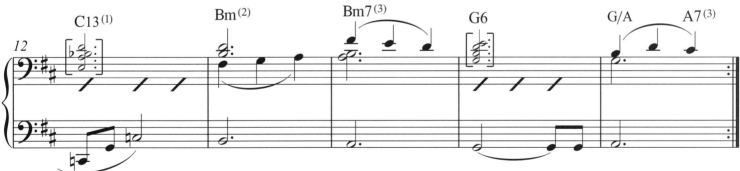

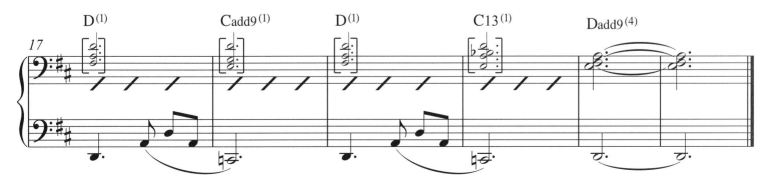

© Novus Via Music Group Inc. 2009. All rights reserved.

Improv Etude - On the Crest

Module 1

Concept: 7 and major 7 chords

A **dominant 7 chord** (also known as a 7 chord) combines a major triad (e.g., D-F♯-A) with a minor 7th above the root (e.g., C♮).

A major 7 chord (**maj7**) is also based on a major triad (e.g., A♭-C-E♭), but adds a major 7th above the root to the chord (e.g., A♭-C-E♭-G).

7 and maj7 chords may be written in **first** and **third inversion**. In a first inversion chord, the third of the

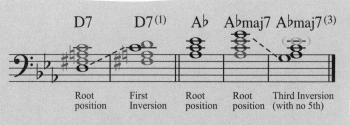

chord is on the bottom. In a third inversion chord, the seventh of the chord is on the bottom.

For improvising on *On the Crest*, the 5th of the maj7 (3) chords will be left out.

A Label the 7 and maj7 chords with their lettername (e.g., D7, G7 or A♭maj7) and a bracketed "1" or "3" for the correct inversion. Practice the left hand first *without*, then *with* the backing track.

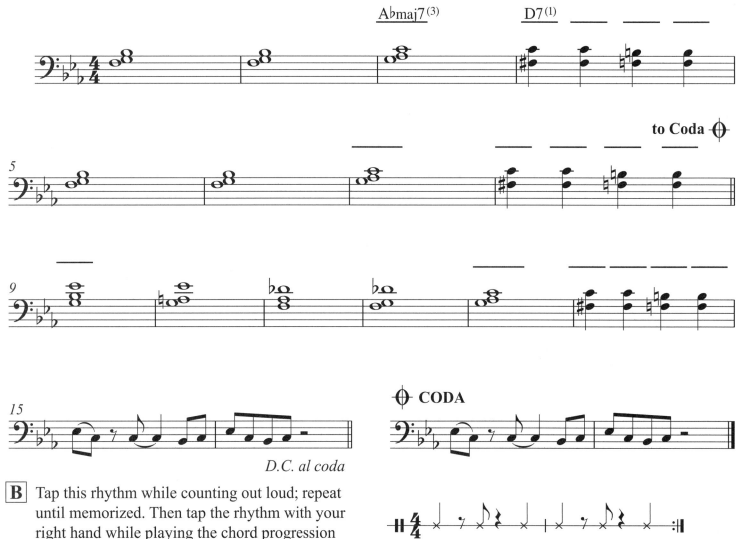

D.C. al coda

B Tap this rhythm while counting out loud; repeat until memorized. Then tap the rhythm with your right hand while playing the chord progression with your left. Finally, make up your own rhythms to go with the left hand chord progression.

© Novus Via Music Group Inc. 2009. All rights reserved.

Improv Tools

To improvise on *On the Crest*, you will use three sets of Improv Notes: one based on the **B♭ Mixolydian mode**, one on the **C Dorian mode**, and one on the **B♭ Dorian mode**.

One way to describe B♭ Mixolydian is as a B♭ Major scale with an A♭ instead of an A♮. One way to describe B♭ Dorian is as a B♭ natural minor scale with a G♮ instead of a G♭.

B♭ Mixolydian mode

B♭ Dorian mode

There are specific Improv Tools you can use to make your improvisation interesting and musical. They can use arpeggio-based ideas.

Call & Response: play an arpeggio-based idea, then "answer" it with a contrasting idea:

Rhythmic Shift: play an arpeggio-based idea and then re-state it starting on a different beat:

C Using the Improv Notes Set A, B, or C as indicated in the score, play various right hand improvisations. Use the Improv Tools, above, to get started. Practice *with* the backing track.

Set A Improv notes:

Set B Improv notes:

Set C Improv notes:

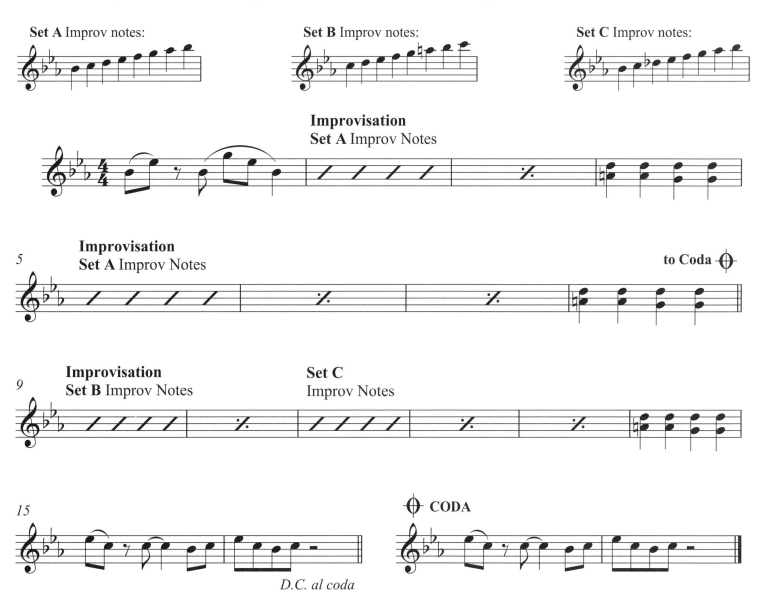

D.C. al coda

© Novus Via Music Group Inc. 2009. All rights reserved.

D Now improvise hands together. Practice first *without*, then *with* the backing track.

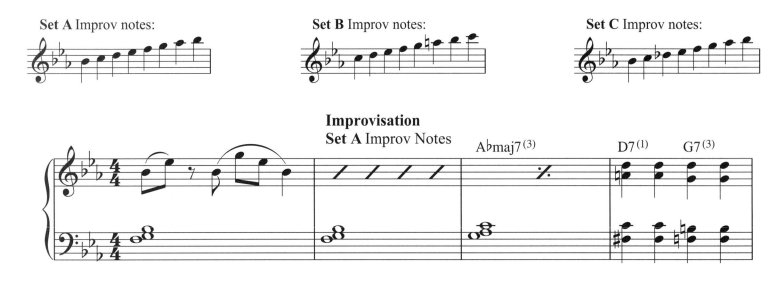

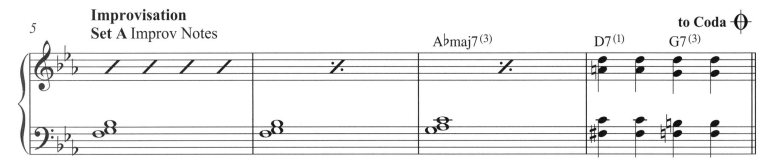

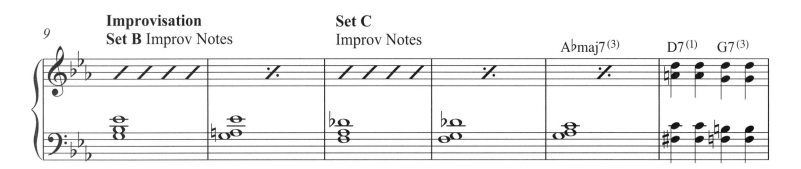

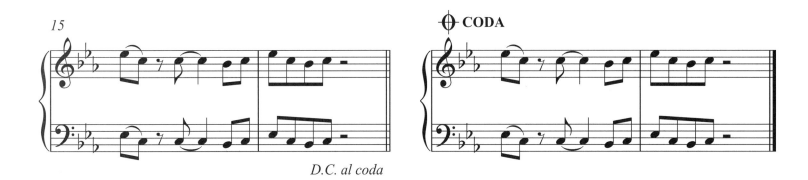

D.C. al coda

✔ **Improv Tip:** *Try using one of the Improv Tools through your whole improvisation.*

© Novus Via Music Group Inc. 2009. All rights reserved.

Vamping Tools

Vamping is an improvised accompaniment often with chords in the right hand against single notes in the left. You can vary blocked right hand chords by changing the pattern of the rhythms.

Right hand rhythmic pattern 1:

Pattern 2:

Pattern 3:

E Vamp various right hand accompaniments using the chords [in brackets] indicated below. Use the Vamping Tools, above, to get started. Practice first *without*, then *with* the backing track.

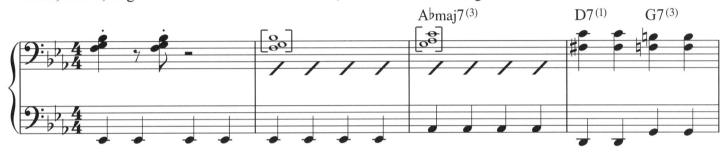

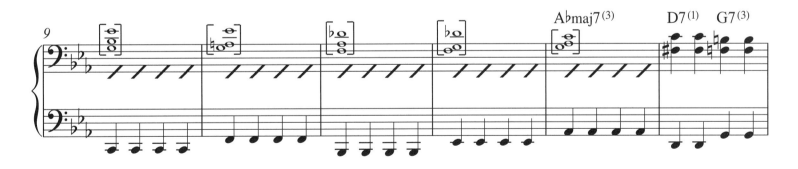

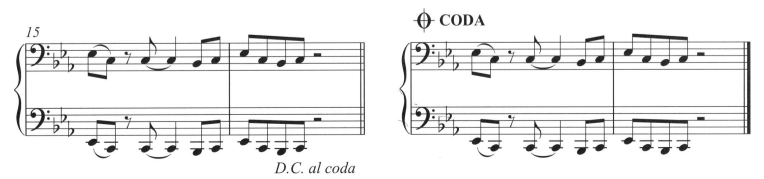

D.C. al coda

© Novus Via Music Group Inc. 2009. All rights reserved.

Improv Etude - On the Crest

Module 2

Concept: minor 7 chords

A **minor 7 chord (m7)** combines a minor triad
(e.g., C-E♭-G) with a minor 7th above the root (e.g., B♭).
Notice this is the same construction as the 7 chord, only
based on a minor triad. Sometimes this is done using all
four notes (e.g., C-E♭-G-B♭), but often it is done using
only three notes to achieve the same sound.

Minor 7 chords may be written in **second inversion**. As
with 7 chords, one way to change a root position m7
chord to second inversion is to take the root and third off

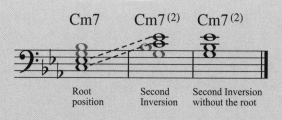

the bottom and move them to the top.

In the *On the Crest* improvisation, the bass notes for
the m7 chords are played in the backing track. In the
Vamp, on page 45, you play them in your left hand.

A Label the second inversion m7 chords with their lettername (e.g., Cm7 or B♭m7) and a bracketed 2 for
"second inversion". Practice the left hand first *without*, then *with* the backing track.

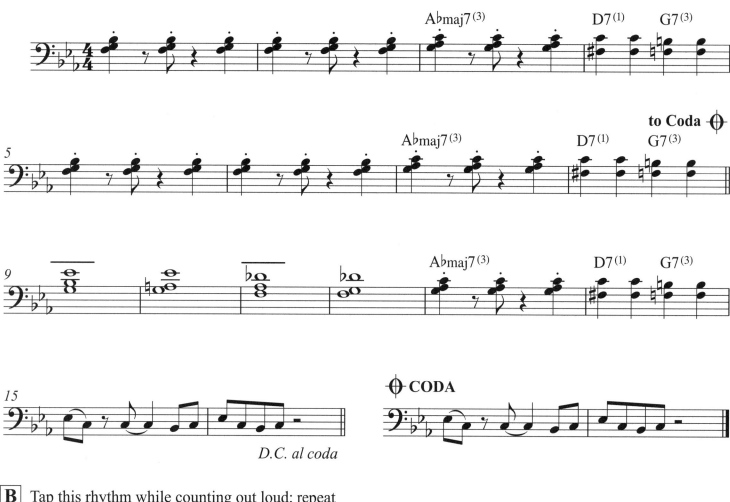

D.C. al coda

B Tap this rhythm while counting out loud; repeat
until memorized. Then tap the rhythm with your
right hand while playing the chord progression
with your left. Finally, make up your own rhythms
to go with the left hand chord progression.

© Novus Via Music Group Inc. 2009. All rights reserved.

Improv Tools

Grace Notes is another Improv Tool you can use, in addition to **Call & Response** and **Rhythmic Shift**.

Your improvisations can also use scale-based ideas.

Call & Response: play a scale-based idea, then "answer" it with a contrasting idea:

Rhythmic Shift: play a scale-based idea and then re-state it starting on a different beat:

Grace Notes: these remain a staple for "spicing up" your improvisation, from above or below the note:

C Using the Improv Notes Set A, B, or C as indicated in the score, play various right hand improvisations. Use the Improv Tools, above and in the previous Module, to get started. Practice *with* the backing track.

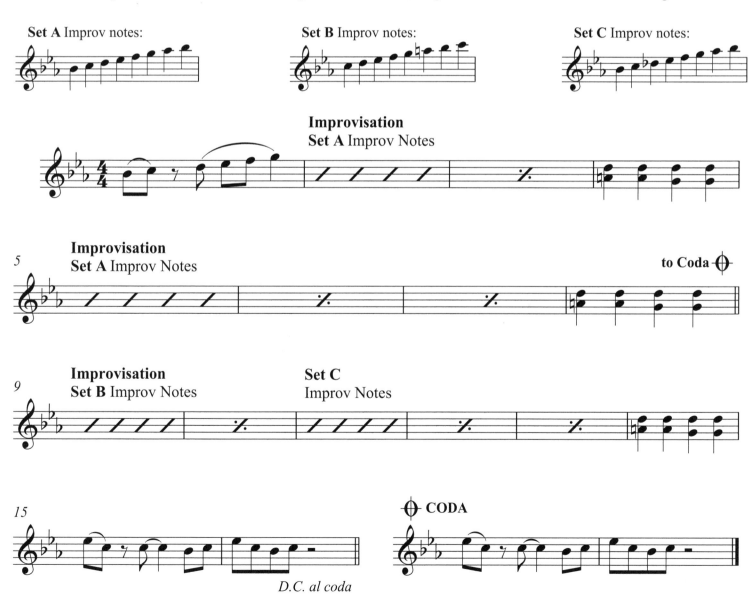

© Novus Via Music Group Inc. 2009. All rights reserved.

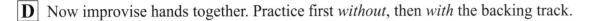

D Now improvise hands together. Practice first *without*, then *with* the backing track.

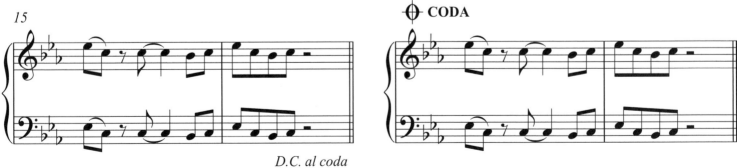

D.C. al coda

✔ Improv Tip: *Try building melodic intensity by putting the highest note at the place you think is the climax.*

© Novus Via Music Group Inc. 2009. All rights reserved.

Vamping Tools

Vamps can also use broken chords in the right hand. You can create interest by varying the starting note of the arpeggiated figure.

Vamp Idea 1 – start from the bottom note of the chord:

Idea 2: start from the top note of the chord:

Idea 3: start from the middle note of the chord:

E Vamp various accompaniments using the chords [in brackets] indicated below. Use the Vamping Tools, above and in the previous Module, to get started. Practice first *without*, then *with* the backing track.

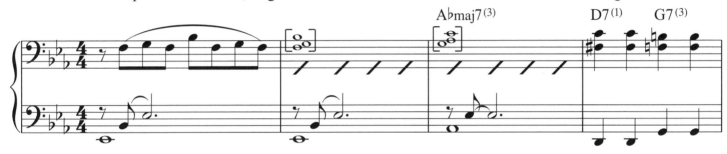

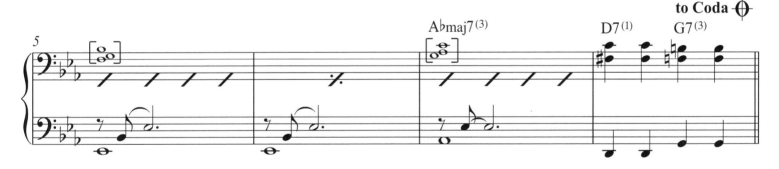

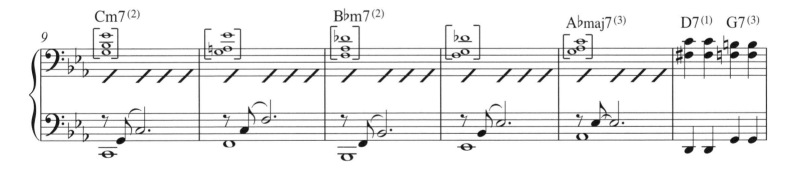

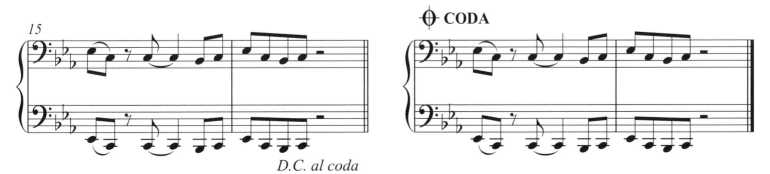

D.C. al coda

© Novus Via Music Group Inc. 2009. All rights reserved.

Improv Etude - On the Crest

Module 3

Concept: 9 & add9 chords

A **9 chord** extends a dominant 7 chord by adding a 9th above the root to the chord. Sometimes this is done using all five notes (e.g., F-A-C-E♭-G), but often it is done using only three notes to achieve the same sound.

When the 7th is to be left out of a chord, this is indicated by saying the 9th is "added". So, an **E♭add9** chord adds a 9th, without the 7th, to an E♭ major triad (E♭-G-B♭-F). 9 and add9 chords may be written in **fourth inversion**. In fourth inversion, the ninth of the

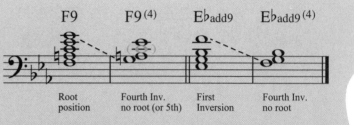

chord is on the bottom.

One way to change a root postion 9 or add9 chord to fourth inversion is to take the 9th off the top and put it on the bottom; you'll also lose the root or move it up an octave.

A Label the 9 and add9 chords with their lettername (e.g., F9 or E♭add9) and a bracketed 4 for "fourth inversion". Practice the left hand first *without*, then *with* the backing track.

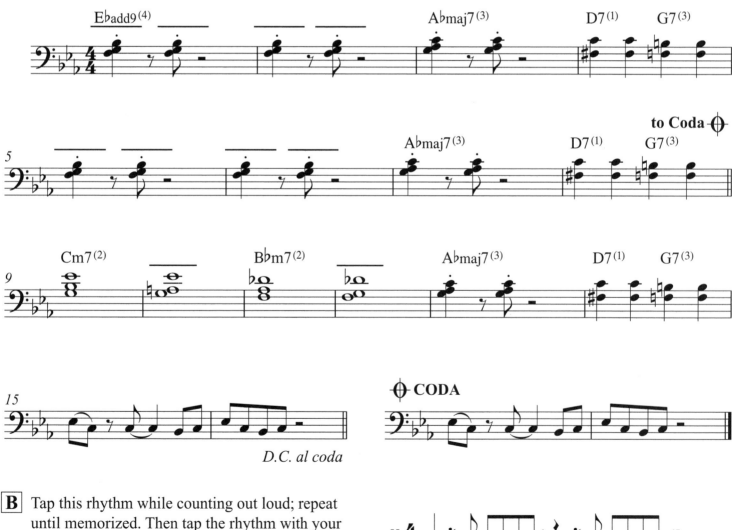

D.C. al coda

B Tap this rhythm while counting out loud; repeat until memorized. Then tap the rhythm with your right hand while playing the chord progression with your left. Finally, make up your own rhythms to go with the left hand chord progression.

© Novus Via Music Group Inc. 2009. All rights reserved.

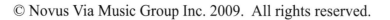

Improv Tools

There are other Improv Tools you can use in your improvisations. Notice how certain Tools can be combined, for example, adding Pedal Notes to a Rhythmic Shift.

Direction Change: start an idea in one direction, up or down, and then change it to move the other way:

Pedal Notes: a pedal note is a repeated note that doesn't change when the melody moves. Here the B♭'s are pedal notes "above":

Idea & Variation: create an idea and then repeat it slightly varied:

C Using the Improv Notes Set A, B, or C as indicated in the score, play various right hand improvisations. Use the Improv Tools, above and in the previous Modules, to get started. Practice *with* the backing track.

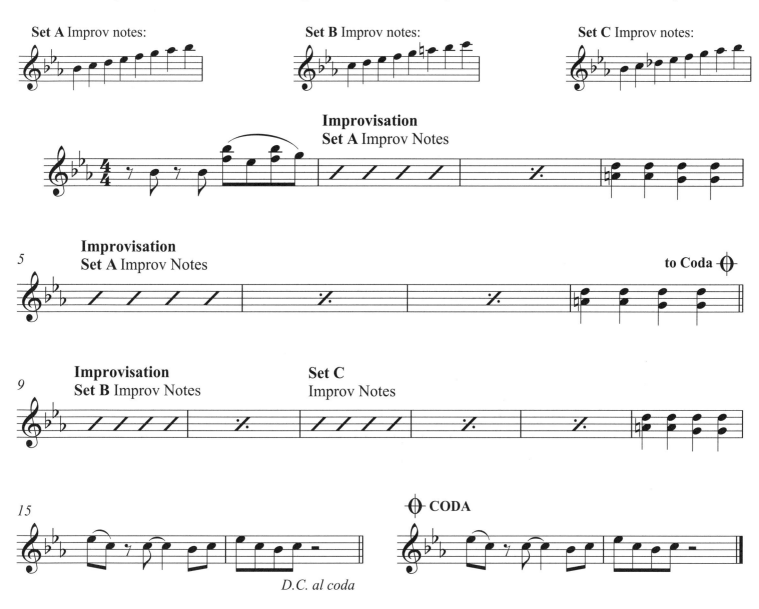

D.C. al coda

© Novus Via Music Group Inc. 2009. All rights reserved.

48

D Now improvise hands together. Practice first *without*, then *with* the backing track.

Improv Tip: *Using Rhythmic Shift to repeat a phrase is a great way of building tension in a solo.*

© Novus Via Music Group Inc. 2009. All rights reserved.

Vamping Tools

There are all kinds of patterns you can create in your vamp using blocked or broken chords, or a combination of the two.

Vamp Idea 1 – using rests to dramatic effect:

Vamp Idea 2: arpeggios followed by blocked chords:

Vamp Idea 3: a driving mix of blocked and broken chords:

E Vamp various accompaniments using the chords [in brackets] indicated below. Use the Vamping Tools, above and in the previous Modules, to get started. Practice first *without*, then *with* the backing track.

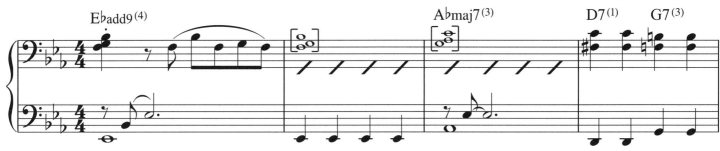

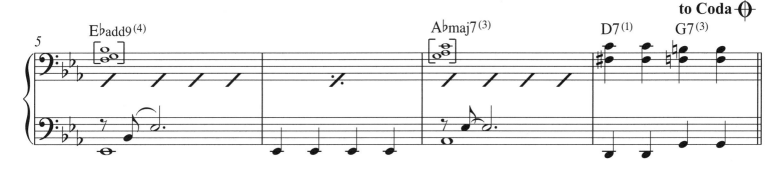

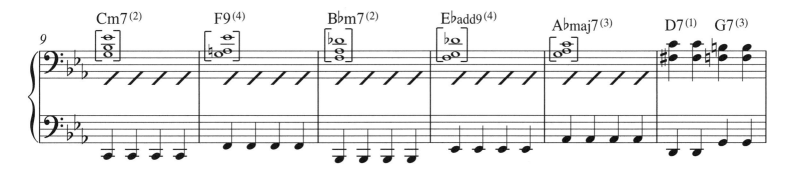

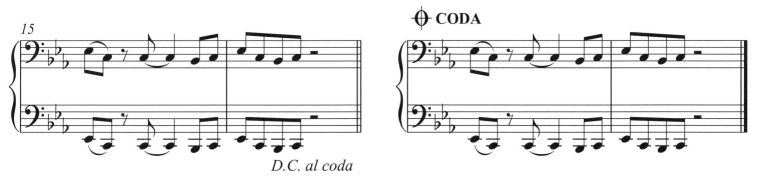

D.C. al coda

© Novus Via Music Group Inc. 2009. All rights reserved.

Improv Etude - A Bird in the Hand

Module 1

Concept: major 6 & minor 7 chords

A **major 6 chord** (also known as a 6 chord) combines a major triad (e.g., C-E-G) with a major 6th above the root (e.g., A). 6 chords may be written in **second inversion**. In second inversion, the fifth of the chord is on the bottom.

A **minor 7 chord (m7)** combines a minor triad (e.g., A-C-E) with a minor 7th above the root (e.g., G). This is the same construction as the 7 chord, only based on a minor triad. Minor 7 chords may also be

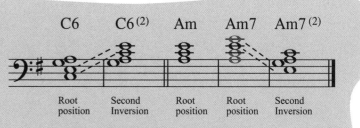

written in **second inversion**.

One way to change a root position chord to second inversion is to take the root and third of the chord off the bottom and move them to the top. Another way is to take the 7th (or 6th) and 5th off the top and move them to the bottom.

A Label the 6 chords and m7 chords with their lettername (e.g., C6, Am7, or Em7) and a bracketed 2 for "second inversion", where appropriate. Practice the left hand first *without*, then *with* the backing track.

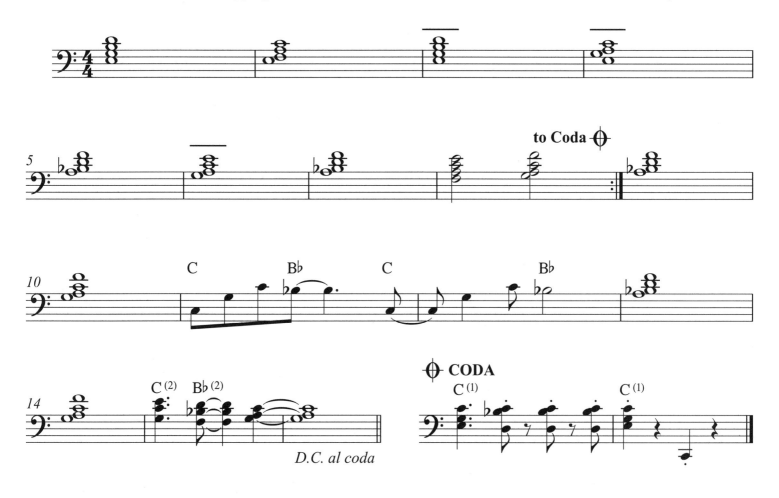

D.C. al coda

B Tap this rhythm while counting out loud; repeat until memorized. Then tap the rhythm with your right hand while playing the chord progression with your left. Finally, make up your own rhythms to go with the left hand chord progression.

© Novus Via Music Group Inc. 2009. All rights reserved.

Improv Tools

To improvise on *A Bird in the Hand*, you will use two sets of Improv Notes: one based on the **G Mixolydian mode**, the other based on the **A Phrygian mode**.

One way to describe G Mixolydian is as a G Major scale with an F♮ instead of an F♯. One way to describe A Phrygian is as an A natural minor scale with a B♭ instead of a B♮.

There are Improv Tools you can use to make your scale-based ideas interesting and musical.

Sequence: play a scale-based idea and then repeat it transposed to start on a different note:

Rhythmic Shift: play a rhythmic figure and then re-state it starting on a different beat. It can be very effective, even using only a few notes:

C Using the Improv Notes Set A or B as indicated in the score, play various right hand improvisations. Use the Improv Tools, above, to get started. Practice *with* the backing track.

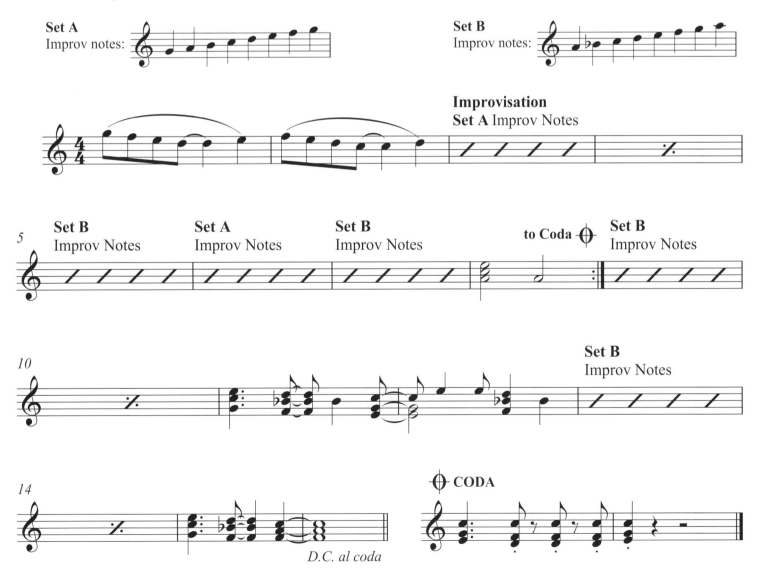

© Novus Via Music Group Inc. 2009. All rights reserved.

D Now improvise hands together. Practice first *without*, then *with* the backing track.

Set A
Improv notes:

Set B
Improv notes:

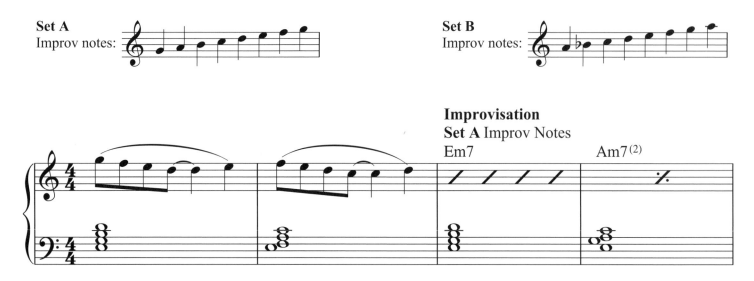

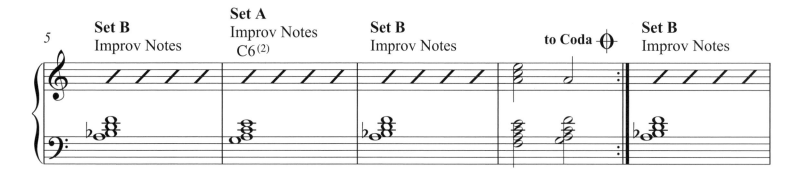

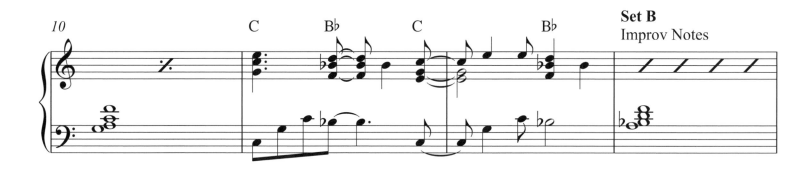

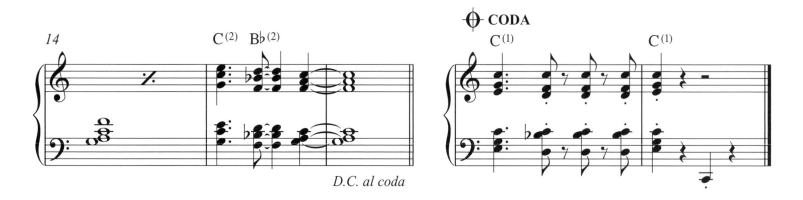

D.C. al coda

✔ **Improv Tip:** *A sequence can be particularly effective when the chord progression moves up or down by one step.*

© Novus Via Music Group Inc. 2009. All rights reserved.

Vamping Tools

Vamping is an improvised accompaniment often with chords in the right hand against single notes in the left. In pieces, such as *A Bird in the Hand*, with a "laid back" feel and rich, full chords, the right hand can focus on providing the harmonic structure.

Right hand rhythmic pattern 1:

Pattern 2 – with a little more rhythmic activity:

Pattern 3 – still more rhythmic activity:

E Vamp various right hand accompaniments using the chords [in brackets] indicated below. Use the Vamping Tools, above, to get started. Practice first *without*, then *with* the backing track.

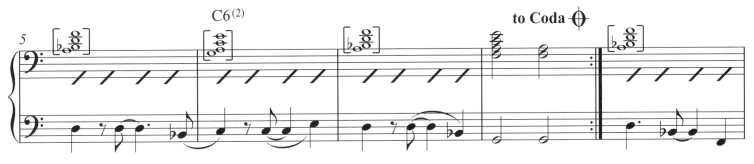

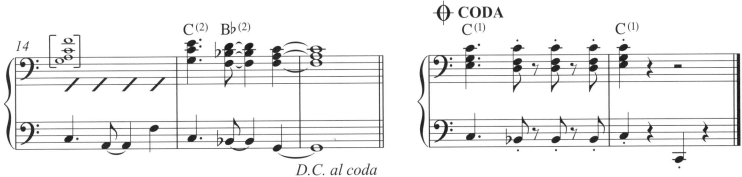

D.C. al coda

© Novus Via Music Group Inc. 2009. All rights reserved.

Improv Etude - A Bird in the Hand

Module 2

Concept: major 7 & split chords

A **major 7 chord** (**maj7**) combines a major triad (e.g., F-A-C) with a major 7 above the root (e.g., E). Sometimes this is done using all four notes (e.g., F-A-C-E). In **third inversion** 7 chords, the seventh is on the bottom.

Split chords can occur when playing chords with both hands. A split chord has a bass note in the left hand that is not the root of the chord – sometimes it is not a note from the chord at all.

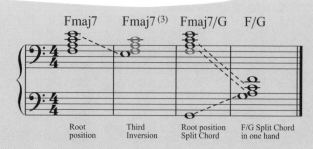

Maj7 chords can be the "top" of a split chord.

In the *A Bird in the Hand* improvisation, the "G" bass note of the Fmaj7/G chords is played in the backing track and with the F/G chords, the sound is created by just the left hand.

A Label the maj7 and split chords with their lettername (e.g., Fmaj7, B♭maj7, F/G, or Fmaj7/G) and a bracketed 3 for "third inversion", as appropriate. Practice the left hand *without*, then *with* the backing track.

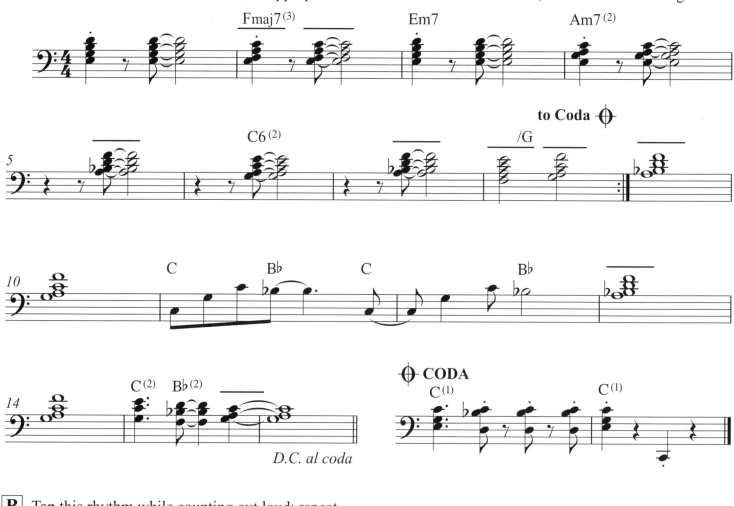

B Tap this rhythm while counting out loud; repeat until memorized. Then tap the rhythm with your right hand while playing the chord progression with your left. Finally, make up your own rhythms to go with the left hand chord progression.

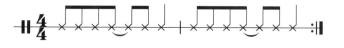

© Novus Via Music Group Inc. 2009. All rights reserved.

Improv Tools

Direction Change is another Improv Tool you can use, in addition to **Sequence** and **Rhythmic Shift**.

Your improvisation can also used arpeggio-based ideas.

Sequence: play an arpeggio-based idea and then repeat it transposed to start on a different note:

Rhythmic Shift: play an arpeggio-based idea and then re-state it starting on a different beat:

Direction Change: play an arpeggio-based idea and then change its direction:

C Using the Improv Notes Set A or B as indicated in the score, play various right hand improvisations. Use the Improv Tools, above and in the previous Module, to get started. Practice *with* the backing track.

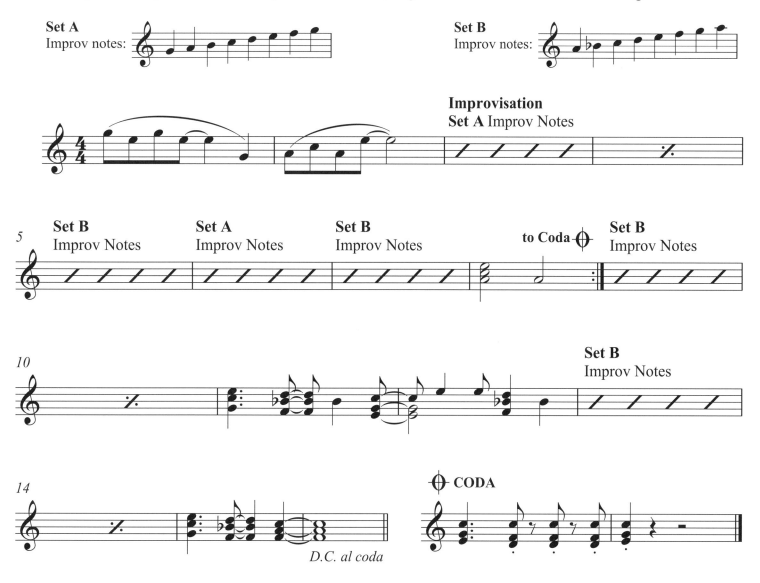

© Novus Via Music Group Inc. 2009. All rights reserved.

D Now improvise hands together. Practice first *without*, then *with* the backing track.

✔ **Improv Tip:** *Try to vary your improvisation by using a mixture of arpeggio-based and scale-based ideas. Don't be timid about using repeated notes, either!*

© Novus Via Music Group Inc. 2009. All rights reserved.

Vamping Tools

Vamps can also use broken chords in the right hand. You can create interest by varying the starting note of the arpeggio.

Vamp Idea 1 – start from the bottom note of the chord:

Idea 2: start from the top note of the chord:

Idea 3: start from the middle note of the chord:

E Vamp various right hand accompaniments using the chords [in brackets] indicated below. Use the Vamping Tools, above and in the previous Module, to get started. Practice first *without*, then *with* the backing track.

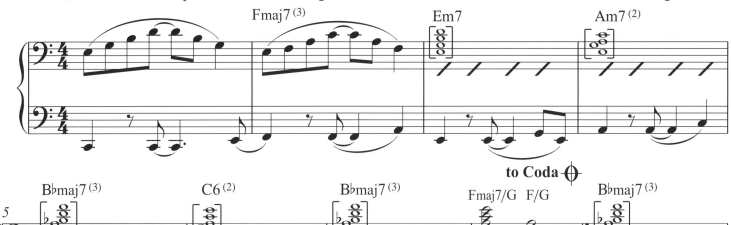

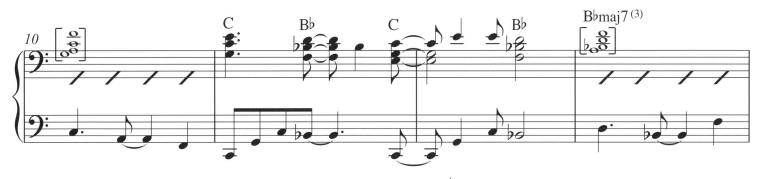

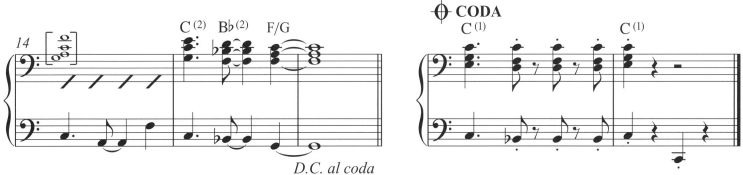

D.C. al coda

© Novus Via Music Group Inc. 2009. All rights reserved.

58

Improv Etude - A Bird in the Hand

Module 3

Concept: major 9 & add9 chords

A **major 9 chord** extends a major 7 chord by adding a 9th above the root to the chord. Sometimes this is done using all five notes (e.g., C-E-G-B-D), but often it is done using fewer notes to achieve the same sound.

When the 7th is to be left out, this is indicated by saying the 9th is "added". So, a **B♭add9** chord adds a 9th, without the 7th, to a B♭ major triad (B♭-D-F-C). 9 and add9 chords may be written in **first inversion**.

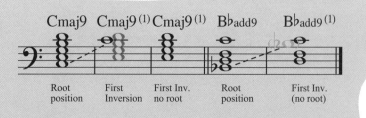

In first inversion, the third of the chord is on the bottom.

In the *A Bird in the Hand* improvisation, the root of the maj9 and add9 chords is played in the backing track. In the Vamp, you play them in your left hand.

A Label the maj9 and add9 chords with their lettername (e.g., Cmaj9, Fadd9, or B♭add9) and a bracketed "1" or "4" for the correct inversion. Practice the left hand first *without*, then *with* the backing track.

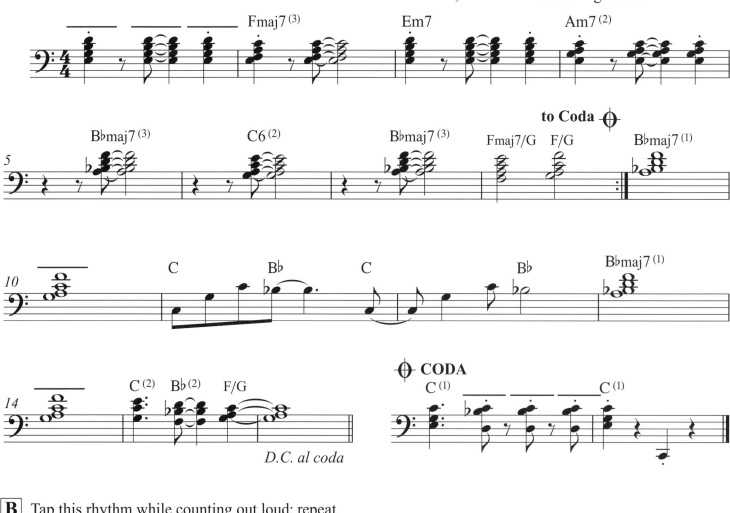

B Tap this rhythm while counting out loud; repeat until memorized. Then tap the rhythm with your right hand while playing the chord progression with your left. Finally, make up your own rhythms to go with the left hand chord progression.

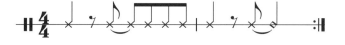

© Novus Via Music Group Inc. 2009. All rights reserved.

Improv Tools

There are other Improv Tools you can use to make your improvisation ideas more interesting and musical.

Idea & Variation: keep the exact rhythm of an idea, but play a completely new set of notes:

Chording: play chords in both hands to create a full, rich sound:

Fourths: play an idea harmonized in fourths:

C Using the Improv Notes Set A or B as indicated in the score, play various right hand improvisations. Use the Improv Tools, above and in the previous Modules, to get started. Practice *with* the backing track.

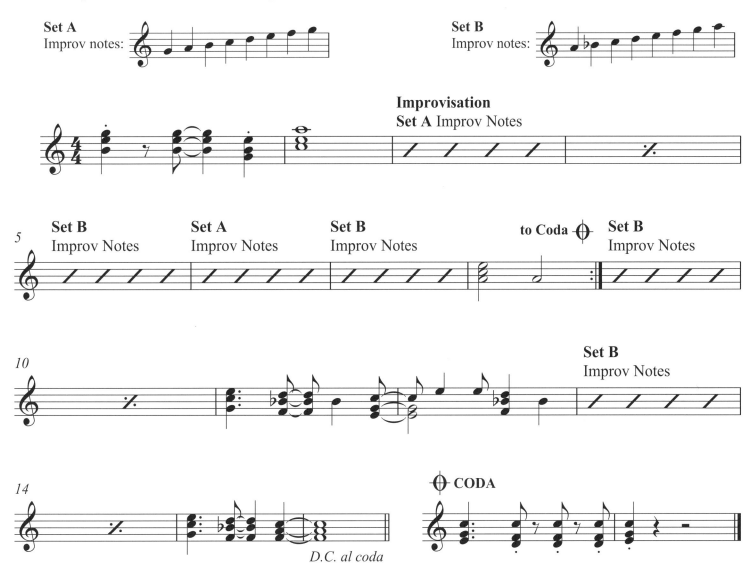

© Novus Via Music Group Inc. 2009. All rights reserved.

D Now improvise hands together. Practice first *without*, then *with* the backing track.

Improv Tip: *Experiment with alternating chording (playing chords in both hands) and single-note melodic lines to create contrasts of texture in your improvisation.*

© Novus Via Music Group Inc. 2009. All rights reserved.

Vamping Tools

Vamps can use a mixture of blocked and broken chords in the right hand. You can create interest by varying the mix, the arpeggios, or the rhythm:

Vamp Idea 1:

Idea 2:

Idea 3:

E Vamp various right hand accompaniments using the chords [in brackets] indicated below. Use the Vamping Tools, above and in the previous Modules, to get started. Practice first *without*, then *with* the backing track.

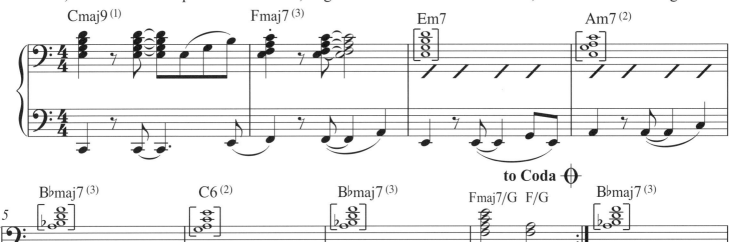

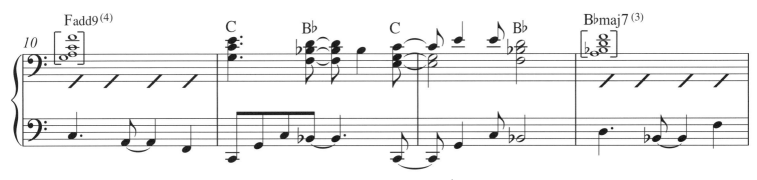

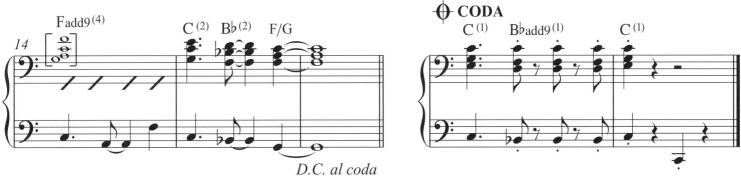

D.C. al coda

© Novus Via Music Group Inc. 2009. All rights reserved.

Improv Etude - Man About Town

Module 1

Concept: Dominant 7, 9, & sus4 chords

A **Dominant 7** (or **7 chord**) combines a major triad (e.g., D-F♯-A) with a minor 7th above the root (e.g., C♮). A **9 chord** is a 7 chord with the addition of the major 9th above the root (e.g., C-E-G-B♭-D). 7 and 9 chords may be written in **first, second**, or **third inversion**. To review changing root position chords to first, second, and third inversion, see Module 1 of *Bayou Tapestry* (pg. 2), *A Bird in the Hand* (pg. 50), and *Lonely Waltz* (pg. 26).

A suspension **sus4 chord** (or a **sus chord**), is created when the fourth degree of a scale is used in a chord

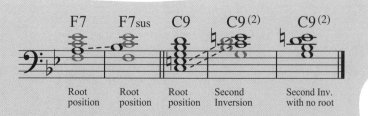

instead of the third degree, "suspending" the resolution we exect to hear. 7 chords may have a suspended fourth. These are known as **7sus** chords.

In the *Man About Town* improvisation, the root of the 9 chords is played in the backing track.

A Label the 7, 9, and 7sus chords with their lettername (e.g., D7, A♭7, C9, G9, or 7sus) and a bracketed "2" or "3" for the correct inversion. Practice the left hand first *without*, then *with* the backing track.

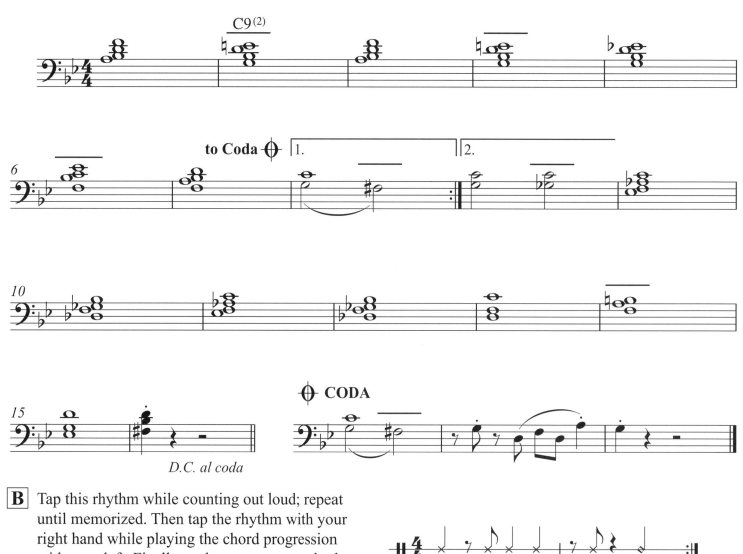

B Tap this rhythm while counting out loud; repeat until memorized. Then tap the rhythm with your right hand while playing the chord progression with your left. Finally, make up your own rhythms to go with the left hand chord progression.

© Novus Via Music Group Inc. 2009. All rights reserved.

Improv Tools

To improvise on *Man About Town*, you will use two sets of Improv Notes: one based on the **G Blues scale**, the other based on the **A♭ major pentatonic scale**.

One way to describe the G Blues scale is as a G **minor pentatonic** (G, B♭, C, D, F♮) with an added D♭. One way to describe the A♭ major pentatonic is as an A♭ Major scale without the 4th or 7th notes.

There are Improv Tools you can use to make your improvisation interesting and musical.

Grace Notes: give your improvisations more character by using grace notes to emphasize certain notes:

Idea & Variation: reuse the exact same notes from an idea, but repeat them with a different rhythm:

C Using the Improv Notes Set A or B as indicated in the score, play various right hand improvisations. Use the Improv Tools, above, to get started. Practice *with* the backing track.

© Novus Via Music Group Inc. 2009. All rights reserved.

64

D Now improvise hands together. Practice first *without*, then *with* the backing track.

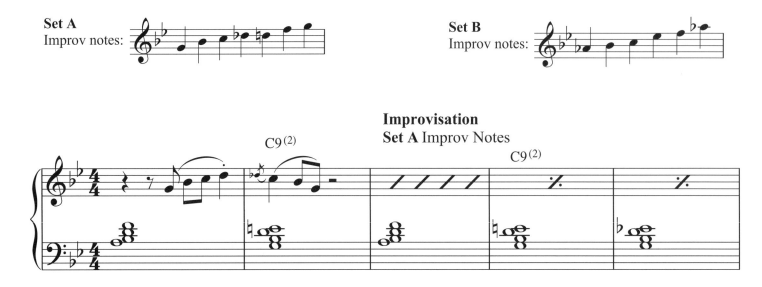

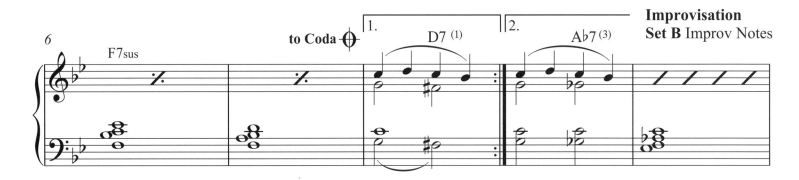

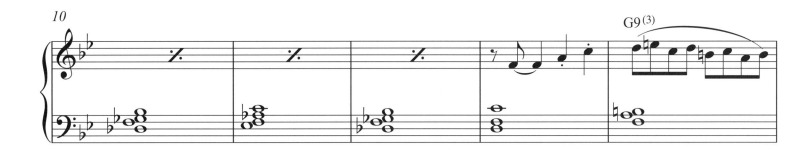

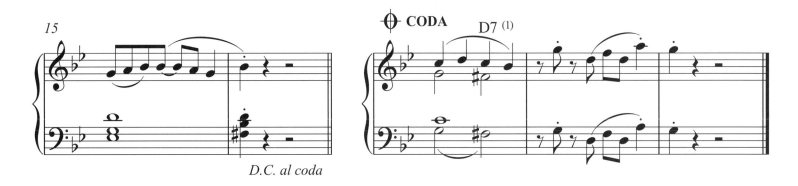

D.C. al coda

✔ **Improv Tip:** *Make an effort to vary the intervals you play in your improvisation to keep it interesting.*

© Novus Via Music Group Inc. 2009. All rights reserved.

Vamping Tools

Vamping is an improvised accompaniment often with chords in the right hand against single notes in the left. You can vary blocked right hand chords by changing the pattern of the rhythms.

Vamp Idea 1 – play with the left hand rhythm, then syncopated to it:

Idea 2 – syncopated to the left hand rhythm:

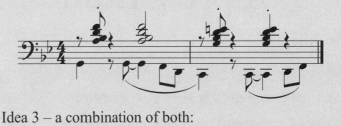

Idea 3 – a combination of both:

E Vamp various right hand accompaniments using the chords [in brackets] indicated below. Use the Vamping Tools, above, to get started. Practice first *without*, then *with* the backing track.

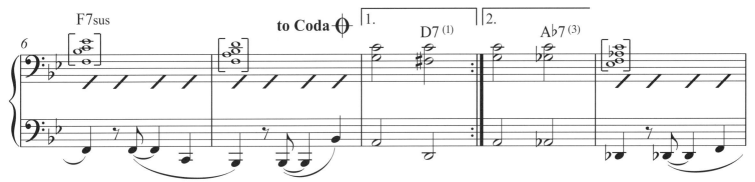

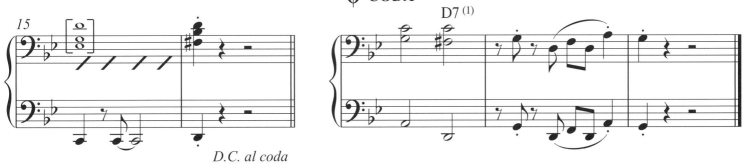

D.C. al coda

© Novus Via Music Group Inc. 2009. All rights reserved.

Improv Etude - Man About Town

Module 2

Concept: minor 7 & minor 9 chords

A **minor 7 chord (m7)** combines a minor triad (e.g., A-C-E) with a minor 7th above the root (e.g., G). This is the same construction as the 7 chord, only based on a minor triad. A **minor 9 chord (m9)** adds a major 9th above the root to the m7 chord (e.g., G-Bb-D-F-A).

Minor 9 chords may be written in **fourth inversion**. In a fourth inversion chord, the ninth of the chord is on the bottom. One way to change a root postion m9 chord to fourth inversion is to take the 9th off the top and put it

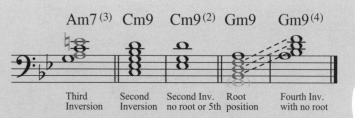

on the bottom; you'll also lose the root or move it up an octave. To review first, second, and third inversion, see Modules 1 & 2 of *On the Crest* (pp. 38 & 42).

In the *Man About Town* improvisation, the root of the m9 chords is played in the backing track.

A Label the m7 and m9 chords with their lettername (e.g., Am7, Dm7, Gm9, or Cm9) and a bracketed "1", "2", "3", or "4" for the inversion, as appropriate. Practice the left hand *without*, then *with* the backing track.

B Tap this rhythm while counting out loud; repeat until memorized. Then tap the rhythm with your right hand while playing the chord progression with your left. Finally, make up your own rhythms to go with the left hand chord progression.

© Novus Via Music Group Inc. 2009. All rights reserved.

Improv Tools

Call & Response is another Improv Tool you can use, in addition to **Grace Notes** and **Idea & Variation**.

Grace Notes: grace notes can add a real sophistication to your improvisation:

Idea & Variation: experiment with rhythmic variations using the same notes from an initial idea:

Call & Response: think up an idea, then "answer" it with a contrasting idea:

C Using the Improv Notes Set A or B as indicated in the score, play various right hand improvisations. Use the Improv Tools, above and in the previous Module, to get started. Practice *with* the backing track.

Set A
Improv notes:

Set B
Improv notes:

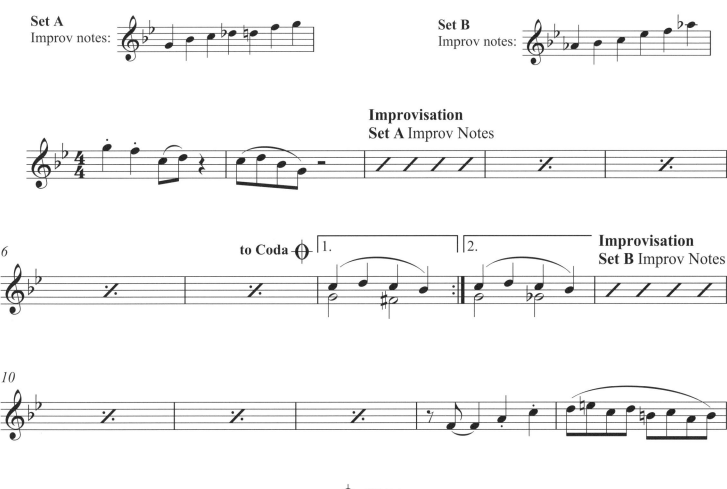

Improvisation
Set A Improv Notes

6

to Coda ⊕ |1. |2.   **Improvisation**
                                       Set B Improv Notes

10

15

D.C. al coda

⊕ **CODA**

© Novus Via Music Group Inc. 2009. All rights reserved.

68

D Now improvise hands together. Practice first *without*, then *with* the backing track.

Set A
Improv notes:

Set B
Improv notes:

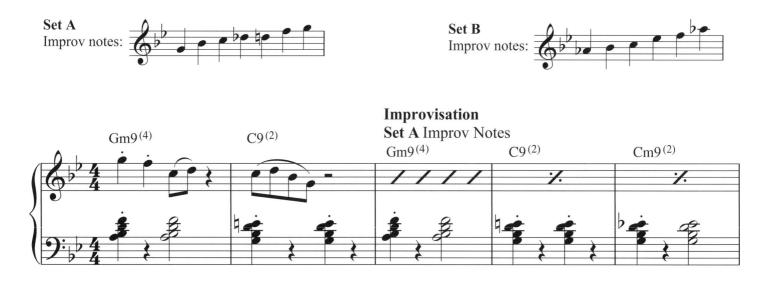

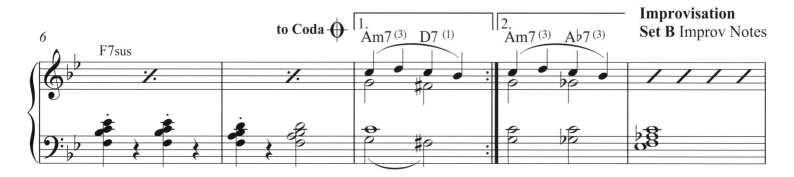

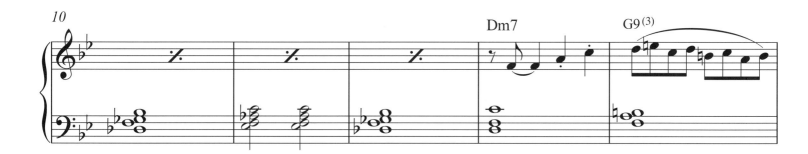

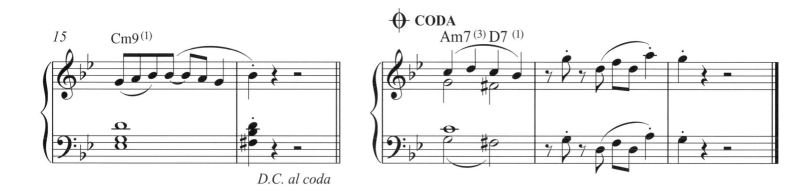

D.C. al coda

✔ **Improv Tip:** *When using the Set A Improv Notes, make a point of accentuating the "blue" note (D♭).*

© Novus Via Music Group Inc. 2009. All rights reserved.

Vamping Tools

Because the chords in *Man About Town* are four-note chords there are even more ways to vary broken chords in your vamp.

Vamp Idea 1:

Idea 2:

Idea 3:

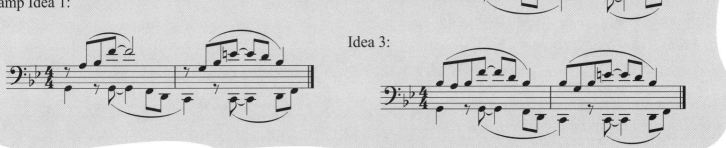

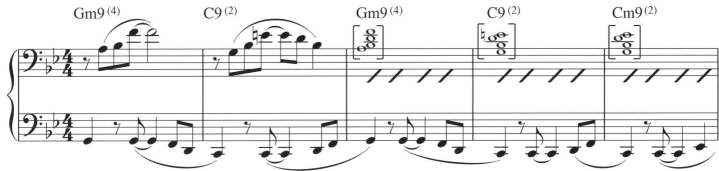

E Vamp various right hand accompaniments using the chords [in brackets] indicated below. Use the Vamping Tools, above and in the previous Module, to get started. Practice first *without*, then *with* the backing track.

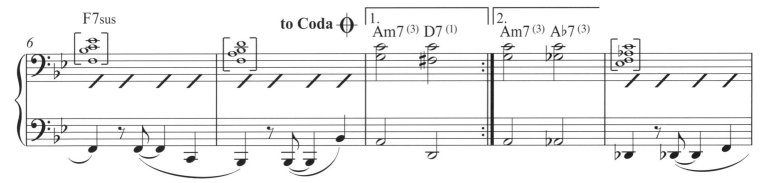

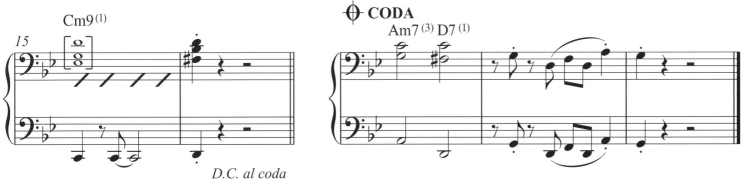

D.C. al coda

© Novus Via Music Group Inc. 2009. All rights reserved.

Improv Etude - Man About Town

Module 3

Concept: major 7 & major 9 chords

A **major 7 chord (maj7)** combines a major triad (e.g., Bb-D-F) with a major 7th above the root (e.g., A). This is the same construction as the 7 chord, only using a major 7th instead of a minor 7th above the root. Similarly, a **major 9 chord (maj9)** adds a 9th above the root to the maj7 chord (e.g., Db-F-Ab-C-Eb).

Major 9 chords may be written in **fourth inversion**. In a fourth inversion chord, the ninth of the chord is on the bottom. One way to change a root postion maj9 chord to fourth inversion is to take the 9th off the top and put

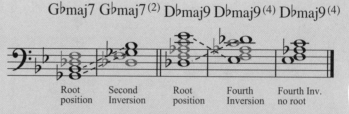

it on the bottom; you'll also lose the root or move it up an octave. To review second inversion, see Module 1 of *A Bird in the Hand* (pg. 50).

In the *Man About Town* improvisation, the root of the maj9(4) chords is played in the backing track.

A Label the maj7 and maj9 chords with their lettername (e.g., Bbmaj7, Gbmaj7, or Dbmaj9) and a bracketed "2" or "4" for the correct inversion. Practice the left hand first *without*, then *with* the backing track.

B Tap this rhythm while counting out loud; repeat until memorized. Then tap the rhythm with your right hand while playing the chord progression with your left. Finally, make up your own rhythms to go with the left hand chord progression.

© Novus Via Music Group Inc. 2009. All rights reserved.

Improv Tools

There are other Improv Tools you can use to make your improvisation more interesting and exciting.

Rhythmic Shift: play an idea and then re-state it starting on a different beat:

Idea & Variation: play an idea and repeat it with a slight variaion (as little as one note!):

Direction Change: if you play an idea that goes up, answer it with one that goes down (or vice versa):

C Using the Improv Notes Set A or B as indicated in the score, play various right hand improvisations. Use the Improv Tools, above and in the previous Modules, to get started. Practice *with* the backing track.

© Novus Via Music Group Inc. 2009. All rights reserved.

D Now improvise hands together. Practice first *without*, then *with* the backing track.

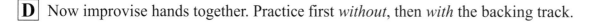

Set A
Improv notes:

Set B
Improv notes:

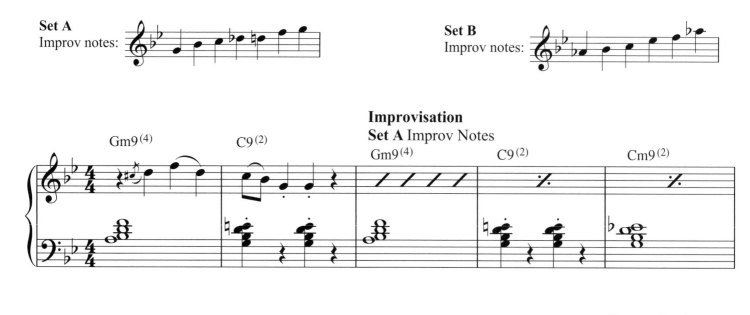

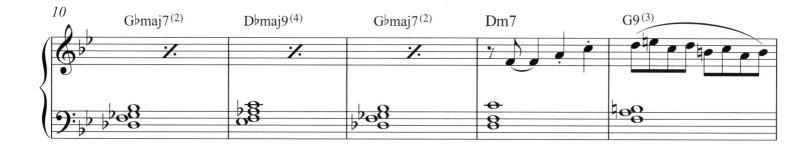

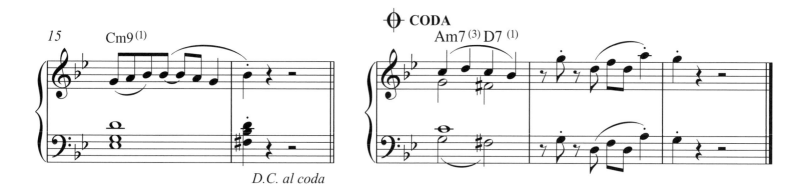

D.C. al coda

✔ **Improv Tip:** *Try using the notated melody as the "idea" in an "idea & variation" to get your improvisation ideas started.*

© novus Via Music Group Inc. 2009. All rights reserved.

Vamping Tools

Vamps can use a mixture of blocked and broken chords in the right hand. You can create interest by varying the mix, the arpeggios, or the rhythm:

Vamp Idea 1:

Idea 2:

Idea 3:

E Vamp various right hand accompaniments using the chords [in brackets] indicated below. Use the Vamping Tools, above and in the previous Modules, to get started. Practice first *without*, then *with* the backing track.

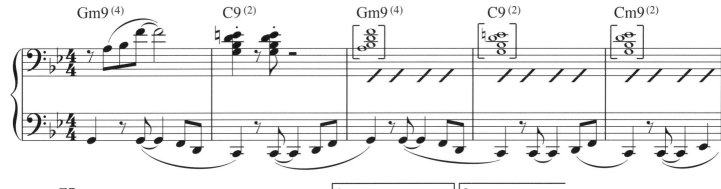

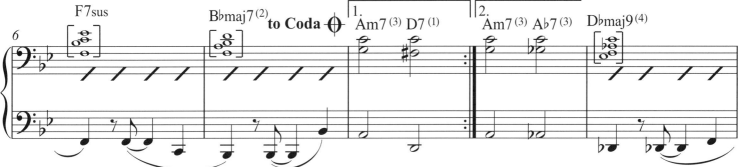

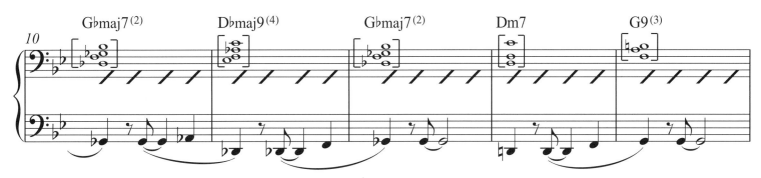

D.C. al coda

© nervus Via Music Group Inc. 2009. All rights reserved.

Allegretto

Carl Czerny

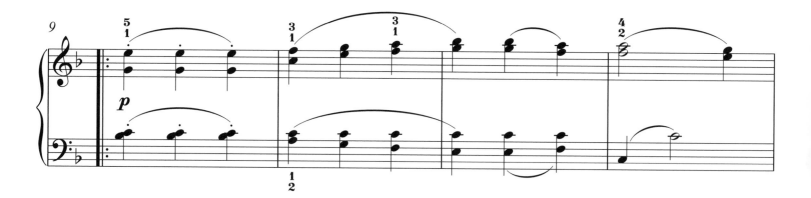

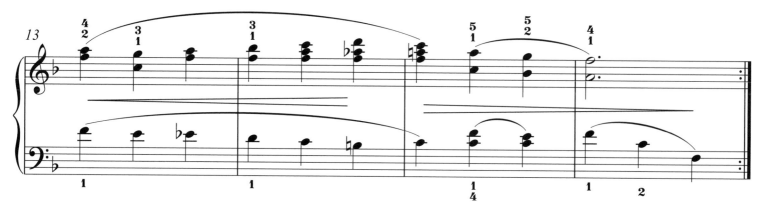

© Novus Via Music Group Inc. 2009. All rights reserved.

Moderato

Henri Herz

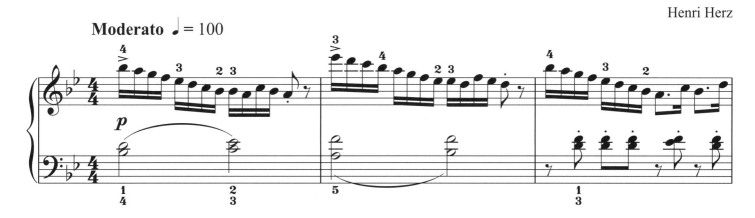

© Novus Via Music Group Inc. 2009. All rights reserved.

Allegretto

Henri Jérôme Bertini

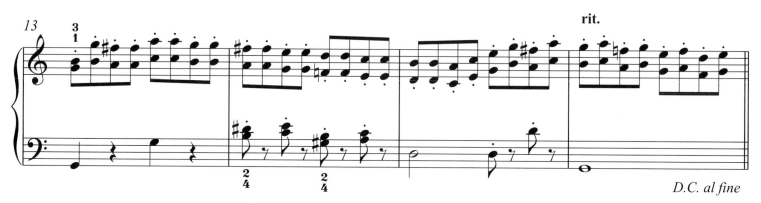

© Novus Via Music Group Inc. 2009. All rights reserved.

Moderato

Carl Czerny

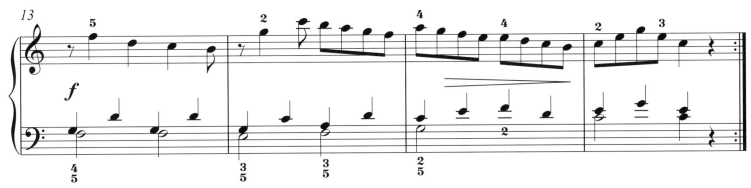

© Novus Via Music Group Inc. 2009. All rights reserved.

A Reproach

Stephen Heller

© Novus Via Music Group Inc. 2009. All rights reserved.

Allegretto

Jean-Baptiste Duvernoy

D.C. al fine

© Novus Via Music Group Inc. 2009. All rights reserved.

Lullaby Blues

Christopher Norton

© Novus Via Music Group Inc. 2009. All rights reserved.

Pacing

Christopher Norton

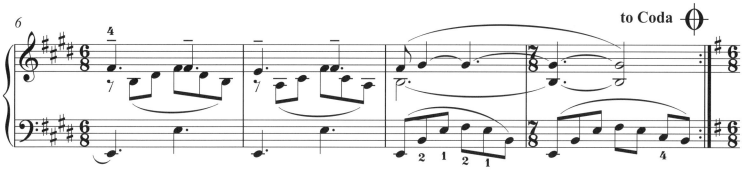

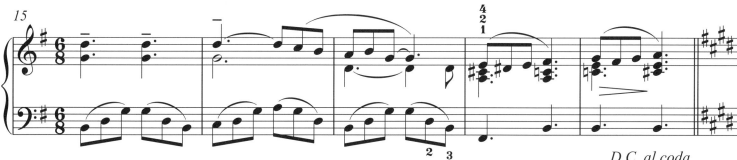

© Novus Via Music Group Inc. 2009. All rights reserved.

Blue Evening

Christopher Norton

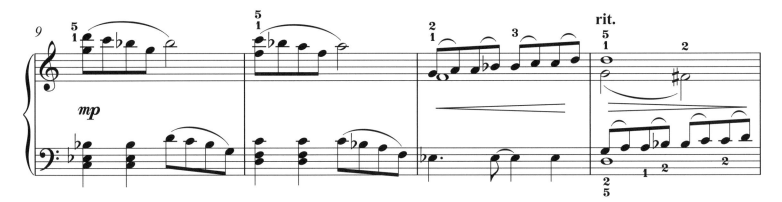

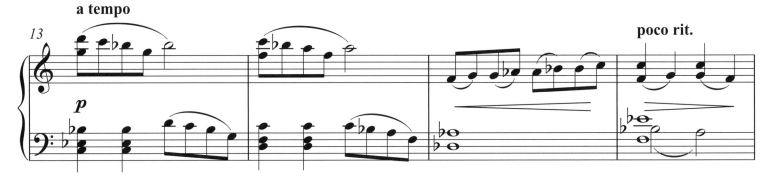

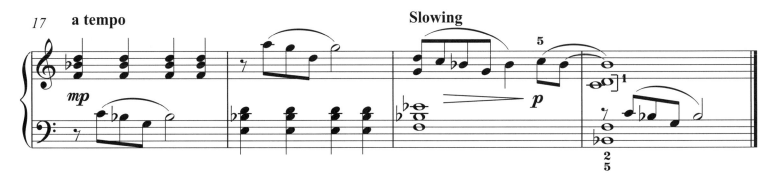

© Novus Via Music Group Inc. 2009. All rights reserved.

Ice Floes

Christopher Norton

© Novus Via Music Group Inc. 2009. All rights reserved.

Twilight

Christopher Norton

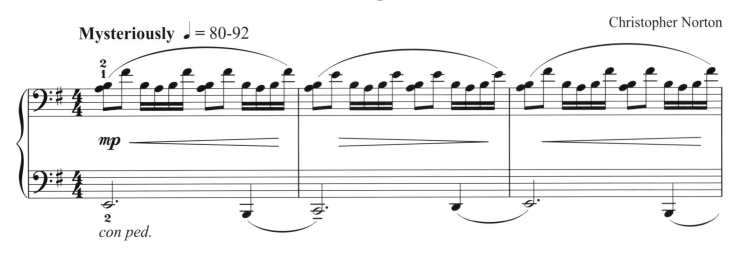

© Novus Via Music Group Inc. 2009. All rights reserved.

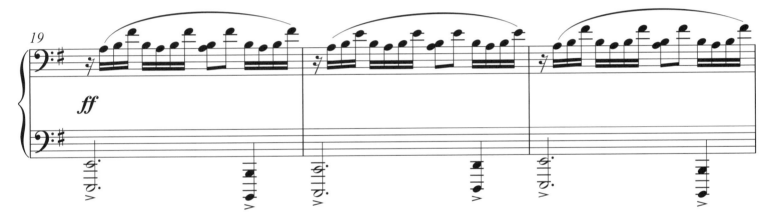

© Novus Via Music Group Inc. 2009. All rights reserved.

LEVEL 7 ETUDES
Glossary

Chord Structures

6 Chords . . . . . . Chords which contain the sixth scale degree above the root.

major 6 . . . . . . Combines a major triad (C-E-G) with the note a major sixth above the root (A). Notated: C6

minor 6 . . . . . . Combines a minor triad (C-E♭-G) with the note a major sixth above the root (A). Notated: Cm6

7 Chords . . . . . . Chords which contain either a major or minor seventh scale degree above the root.

dominant 7 . . Also known as a "7 chord". A major triad (C-E-G) combined with the note a minor 7th above the root (B♭). Notated: C7

major 7 . . . . . . Combines a major triad (C-E-G) with the note a major seventh above the root (B). Notated: Cmaj7

minor 7 . . . . . . A minor triad (C-E♭-G) combined with the note a minor seventh above the root (B♭). Notated: Cm7

9 Chords . . . . . . Extended chords which contain the major ninth scale degree above the root

dominant 9 . . Also known as a "9 chord". A 7 chord (C-E-G-B♭) with an added major ninth on top (C-E-G-B♭-D). Notated: C9

major 9 . . . . . . Adds a ninth above the root to the maj7 chord (C-E-G-B-D). Notated: Cmaj9

minor 9 . . . . . . A minor 7 chord (C-E♭-G-B♭) with an added major ninth above the root (D). Notated: Cm9

13 Chords . . . . . Extended chords which contain the major 13th scale degree above the root.

dominant 13 . Also known as a "13 chord". A 7 chord (C-E-G-B♭) with an added major 9th, 11th, and 13th above the root (D, F, A an octave above). Usually the 11th and sometimes the 9th are omitted. Notated: C13

Add Chords . . Indicates a note above the octave is added to a non-7 chord, without including every chord note in between. See Extended Chords.

add9 . . . . Starts with a triad (C-E-G) and adds the note a ninth above the root (D). Notated: Cadd9

m6add9 . . . . Starts with a m6 chord (C-E♭-G-A) and adds a ninth above the root to the chord (D). Notated: Cm6add9

Augmented Chords . . . A major chord in which the fifth is raised a half step (C-E-G♯). Notated: Caug

7aug . . . . A 7 chord in which the fifth is raised a half step (C-E-G♯-B♭). Notated: C7aug

Close Position . . . . When the notes of a chord are arranged as close together as possible (C major triad played C-E-G).

Extended Chords . . . . . . Indicates a note or notes above the octave are added to a 7 chord; could include every chord note in between (9, 11, or 13 chords). See Added Chords.

Inversions . . . . . Chords in which the root is not on the bottom.

first . . . . The third of a chord (the note E in a C major chord of C) is at the bottom of a chord (E-G-C). Notated: C⁽¹⁾

second . . . . The fifth of a chord (the note G in a C major chord of C) is at the bottom of a chord (G-C-E). Notated: C⁽²⁾

third . . . . The seventh of a chord (the note B♭ in a C7 chord) is at the bottom of a chord (B♭-C-E-G). Notated: C7⁽³⁾

fourth . . . . When the ninth of a chord (the note D in a C9 chord) is at the bottom of a chord (D-E-G-B♭-C). Notated: C9⁽⁴⁾

Root Position . . . . When a chord is written line-line-line (line-line) or space-space-space (space-space), it is in root position. The root is the bottom note.

Split Chords . . Chords which contain a bass note which is not the root of the chord. Often the bass note is not a note from the chord at all.

major 7 . . . . . . Puts a maj7 chord in the right hand (C-E-G-B) over a bass note in the left hand, usually down at least one octave, other than the root (D). Notated: Cmaj7/D

minor 7 . . . . . . Puts a m7 chord in the right hand (C-E♭-G-B♭) over a bass note in the left hand, usually down at least one octave, other than the root (B♭). Notated: Cm7/B♭

major 6 . . . . . . Combines a maj6 chord in the right hand (C-E-G-A) over a bass note in the left hand, usually down at least one octave, other than the root (D). Notated: C6/D

Sus4 Chords . . Also known as a "sus" chord. When a triad is written using the fourth degree of the scale instead of the third, the fourth is said to be "suspending" the expected resolution to the third.

7sus . . . . Raises the third of a 7 chord to the fourth (C-F-G-B♭). Notated: C7sus

Melodic Structures

Blues scale . . . . A six-note blues scale consists of a minor pentatonic scale with the addition of a flatted fifth (or sharpened fourth) scale degree (C-E♭-F-G♭-G-B♭).

Modes . . . . Scales with names drawn from the ancient Greeks, used in folk, pop, and some classical pieces.

Dorian . . . . A seven-note scale with half steps between scale degrees 2-3 and 6-7 (C-D-E♭-F-G-A-B♭-C).

Lydian . . . . A seven-note scale with half steps between scale degrees 4-5 and 7-8 (C-D-E-F♯-G-A-B-C).

Mixolydian . . A seven-note scale with half steps between scale degrees 3-4 and 6-7 (C-D-E-F-G-A-B♭-C).

Phrygian . . . . . A seven-note scale with half steps between scale degrees 1-2 and 5-6 (C-D♭-E♭-F-G-A♭-B♭-C).

Pentatonic . . . . A five-note scale based on the first five notes of the overtone series (C-G-D-A-E), arranged in scale form (C-D-E-G-A).

major . . . . A common form of this five-note scale uses scale degrees 1-2-3-5-6 of a major scale (C-D-E-G-A).

minor . . . . A common form of this five-note scale uses scale degrees 1-3-4-5-7 of a natural minor scale (C-E♭-F-G-B♭).

Terms & Symbols

Licks . . . . Short, catchy melodic motifs, often used to describe guitar playing.

Motif . . . . A group of notes that form a musical idea.

Ostinato . . . . A rhythmic or melodic pattern repeated at length in one voice.

Repeat

full bar . . . . Repeat the entire previous measure.

double full bar . . . . repeat the entire previous two measures.

Riff . . . . Another term for ostinato, often used in pop music. A repeated pattern of notes, chord progression, or rhythmic pattern, often played by the rhythm section.

Slash notation . . . . Signals performers to create their own rhythmic pattern. A slash is placed over each beat.

Tremolo . . . . A fast alternation between two notes, notated by strokes on the stem of the notes, or between the stems of the notes.